I. Northern Wales

National Trust Walks

Walks

I. Northern Wales

Dafydd Meirion

First published in 2006

© Text: Dafydd Meirion
© Photographs: Dafydd Meirion/Gwasg Carreg Gwalch

ISBN: 1-84524-061-8

Published by
Llygad Gwalch,
Ysgubor Plas, Llwyndyrys, Pwllheli, Gwynedd, Wales, LL53 6NG.
Tel: 01758 740432
e-mail: gai@llygadgwalch.com
www.llygadgwalch.com

The author nor the publishers takes any responsibility
if you are injured or if you – against advice given – are caught trespassing.

DAFYDD MEIRION

A former journalist from Dyffryn Nantlle near Caernarfon. He has already had published *Walking Anglesey's Shoreline* and *Walking Llŷn's Shoreline* as well as four novels in Welsh, four walking books for the family, *Anturio ym Môn, Anturio yn Llŷn, Anturio yn Eryri* and *Anturio yn y Cymoedd* (the first having been translated into English as *Walking Adventures in Anglesey*), *Welsh Cowboys and Outlaws*, the history of the Welsh in the American Wild West, and a book on Welsh pirates.

Introduction

With the publication of this book, the National Trust marks another important landmark in its history. Without doubt, one of the best ways to appreciate our houses and landscapes is to visit them on foot, to admire them at leisure and savour their unique atmosphere.

The number of National Trust properties has increased over the years, especially in rural areas and it is more important now than ever to ensure rural communities enjoy a prosperous future by safeguarding what is currently in place, and supporting suitable developments for the future. This can be achieved by working with a number of agencies on a national level but also through creative initiatives, such as the publication of this book, which will enable ramblers to enjoy the countryside and take pleasure from the warm welcome and hospitality offered to them by local people.

The National Trust is not just a guardian of historic houses; it is an organisation which protects a substantial part of Wales' mountains, valleys, beaches and coastlines. The public have been generous in their support of appeals for money and as a result the National Trust's property portfolio has increased dramatically. One example of this is the Neptune Coastline Campaign, launched forty-one years ago in a bid to buy parts of coastline under threat. As a direct result of this appeal, the National Trust now protects 140 miles of beautiful coastline and beaches which are free from any unsuitable commercial threat and available for all to enjoy.

The land and properties under the National Trust's protection are among our greatest national assets. They include open spaces as well as buildings, which show clearly how man's love for his home, be it a palace or a cottage has evolved over the course of time. Needless to say, these are beautiful places to behold but the National Trust is aware of the need to take further steps. Every effort is now made to explain how our environment originated and evolved, whether it be natural or of man's making. It is imperative that we can interpret and understand our past and present before we can lay firm foundations for the future.

And that is the great benefit of this book. By leading us to so many of the National Trust's treasures, we are given a remarkable and revealing glimpse of Welsh landscape, heritage and culture.

Iwan Huws, Director of the National Trust in Wales

WALKING

Places of historical interest are printed in **bold** with details included at the end of each walk. These are only short notes; for more information there are numerous books on the area.

These are all circular routes and none should take more than four and a half hours. All have car parks near the starting point and most have bus stops nearby. Leaflets with the latest bus times can be found in various tourist information offices or by phoning Traveline Cymru on 0870 608 2608. If you wish to visit some of the properties, it is advisable for you phone to check when they are open – especially in winter (the telephone number is given near the name of the attraction).

WHAT TO WEAR

It is advisable to wear walking boots for these walks and if you want to avoid blisters two thick pairs of socks. Although it depends what time of year that you do the walks, it is always advisable to take warm clothes with you, even on a sunny summer day when the wind can often be very cold. It is preferable to have layers of clothing that you can take off as you warm up. If you are walking in cold weather, it is also advisable to take a warm, woolly hat and gloves

You will be very fortunate if you do not encounter any rain. Take with you wet weather clothing, including over-trousers.

A simple map is included with the details of each walk and these should be sufficient, but if you do want to take a map with you, I recommend the *1:25,000 OS Explorer* maps. The maps required are listed on the Contents page.

Readers are advised that whilst every effort is taken by the author to ensure the accuracy of this guidebook, changes can occur which may affect the contents. It is advisable to check details locally before and during each walk.

THE COUNTRY CODE
Guard against any risk of fire.
Keep to the public rights of way when crossing farmland.
Avoid causing any damage to walls, fences and hedges.
Leave farm gates as you find them.
Keep dogs under control and on leads in the presence of livestock.
Leave machinery, farm animals and crops alone.
Take care not to pollute water.
Carry your litter home with you.
Protect all wildlife, plants and trees.
Avoid making any unnecessary noise.
Drive carefully on country roads.
Enjoy and respect the countryside.

PLACE-NAMES
Very few place-names have an English equivalent. When there are, these are given in brackets. To help you understand what some of these place names mean, here is a list of Welsh words. They are often followed by the names of saint or prince or topographical feature, e.g. Aberdaron – the mouth of the river Daron.

Aber – *estuary, river mouth*
Afon – *river*
Allt (Gallt) – *slope*
Bach (Fach) – *small*
Barcud – *kite*
Bedd – *grave*
Bron – *breast of a hill*
Bryn – *hill*
Bwlch – *pass*
Cae – *field*
Caer – *fort*
Capel – *chapel*
Carn – *cairn*
Carreg – *rock, stone*

Castell – *castle*
Coch – *red*
Coed – *wood*
Cors (Gors) – *bog, marsh*
Craig – *rock*
Croes – *cross*
Cromlech – *burial chamber*
Cwm – *valley*
Dinas – *fort*
Dôl/Ddôl – *meadow*
Du/Ddu – *black*
Dŵr – *water*
Dyffryn – *valley*
Eglwys – *church*

Ffordd – *road*
Ffynnon – *spring, well*
Gefail (Efail) – *smithy*
Glan – *river bank*
Glas – *blue, green*
Gwyn – *white*
Gwynt – *wind*
Hafod – *summer dwelling*
Hen – *old*
Hendre – *winter dwelling*
Heulog – *sunny*
Hir – *long*
Isaf – *lower*
Llan – *church*
Llyn – *lake*
Llys – *court, palace*
Maen – *stone*
Maes – *field*
Mawr (Fawr) – *big, great, large*
Melin – *mill*
Moel (Foel) – *bare hill*
Morfa – *sea marsh*
Mynachdy – *monastery*
Mynydd – *mountain*
Nant – *stream*
Newydd – *new*
Ogof – *cave*
Pant – *hollow*
Parc – *park, field*
Pen – *head, top*
Penrhyn – *promontory, headland*
Pentir – *headland*
Pentre – *village*
Plas – *mansion*
Pont – *bridge*
Porth – *port, entrance*

Pwll – *pool*
Rhos – *moorland*
Rhyd – *ford*
Tafarn – *inn*
Traeth – *beach*
Tref – *town*
Trwyn – *promontory*
Twr – *tower*
Ty – *house*
Tyddyn – *small farm, smallholding*
Uchaf – *upper*
Y (Yr) – *the*
Ynys – *island*

And if you want to greet someone in Welsh –
Bore da – *good morning*
Pnawn da – *good afternoon*
Noswaith dda – *good evening*
Os gwelwch yn dda – *please*
Diolch – *thank you*

9

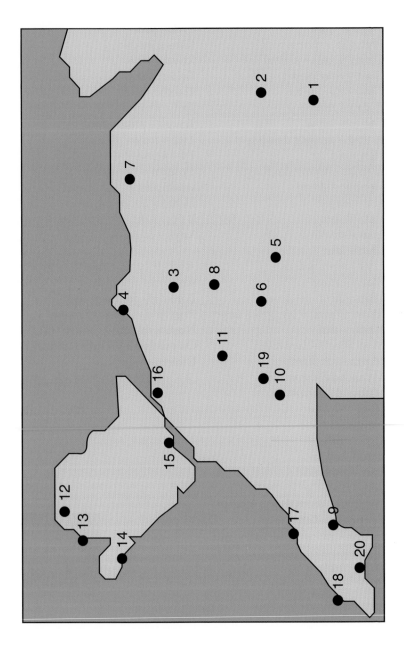

The Routes

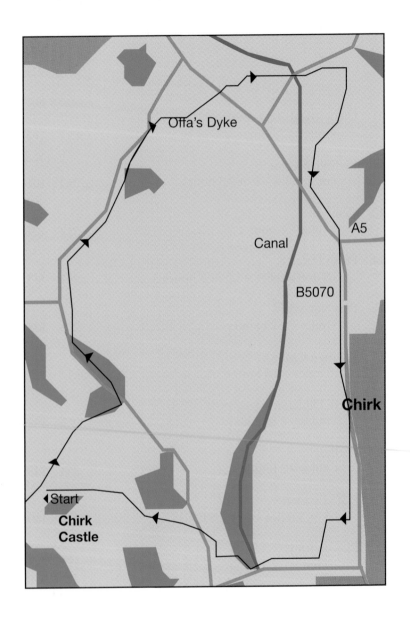

Offa's Dyke

A5

Canal

B5070

Chirk

Start

Chirk
Castle

I. CHIRK CASTLE
Tel. 01691 777701

Chirk Castle

Completed in 1310 by Roger Mortimer, it has been continually occupied for seven centuries. The castle houses elegant state rooms with elaborate plasterwork, Adam-style furniture and tapestries and portraits. Features from different eras include the medieval tower and dungeon and an 18th century servants' hall. The Long Gallery is more than a hundred feet long with its classical decorations dating back to 1672. In the formal garden are clipped yews, roses and climbers on the castle walls. Further on, the garden is less formal, with a thatched hawk house and rock garden. The shrub garden has a small pool and rare varieties of trees and shrubs. A terrace leads to a classical pavilion and 17th century lime tree avenue. The 18th century parkland contains many mature trees. London merchant Sir Thomas Myddelton bought the castle in 1595 and it stayed in the family's possession for nearly 400 years.

The impressive gates to the castle were commissioned by Sir Richard Myddleton and were constructed by the brothers

Robert and John Davies of Bersham near Wrexham between 1712 and 1719. At first they were installed in front of the castle facing north, but they were moved to the New Hall entrance in 1770 and to the present position in 1888.

The walk – *from Chirk Castle along part of Offa's Dyke, and then following part of the Shropshire Union Canal, through Chirk and back to the Castle.*
8.5 miles – 3 hours

Park your car in the Chirk Castle car park (the gates close at 6.30, therefore make sure that you can return by this time). There isn't a bus service to the Castle but if you are not coming by car you can start and finish the walk from Chirk. Go out of the car park and down along the lane that you drove along to get to the Castle car park and down to the entrance. Go to the left through the trees and up the hill. Then down the hill and up again and to a junction. Go straight ahead and past Caeau Gwynion on your right. Ignore the stile on the left and you will then reach a sign with an image of an acorn on it on the left. You are now on the Offa's Dyke Path.

Continue along the road. You will then go past a house on the right and then see another sign with an acorn on it pointing down a narrow lane. Go down the lane, under the trees to a junction. Go straight ahead and up the hill.

You will then see another acorn sign and a stile on the right. Go over the stile and go straight ahead with the fence on your right. Go right following the fence and across the field aiming for a gap. (If the grass has grown high or if there are crops in the field, go around the edge.) In the gap you will see another acorn sign on the left and a stile. Go over the stile and go straight ahead alongside the hedge and you will reach a sign and a stone stile.

Go over the stile and out into the road. Cross the road and go to the right and then you will see a footpath sign on the left.

Part of Offa's Dyke

Follow the track up through the trees. To your right is a part of **Offa's Dyke**. You will then reach a gate and stile. Go over the stile and go straight ahead alongside Offa's Dyke to the corner of the field with a footpath sign and stile. Go over the stile and then over Offa's Dyke to another stile. Go over it and straight ahead; to your left is the Llangollen branch of the **Shropshire Union Canal.** Continue straight ahead to the far end of the field where there is a bridge over the canal and a footpath sign and a stile. Go over the stile and into the road.

Turn to the left, over the bridge and up the road to your right to Pentre. Go past the school on the left and to a footpath sign and kissing gate on the right. Walk through the gate and continue to another kissing gate. Go through it and continue to a gate. Go through this and continue to a stile and a gate. Go over the stile and straight ahead with the fence to another gate. Go through the gate and keep to the right and you will reach a kissing gate and a gate. Go through the kissing gate and out into

Barge on the Llangollen branch of the Shropshire Union Canal

a lane. Keepto the left and up the hill and you will reach the main road.

Turn to the left and go down the road. Cross the road before you reach the roundabout and go to the right and up the hill into **Chirk**. Go past the Kronospan factory entrance on the right and past the police station and church on the left. Go past another Kronospan entrance and you will see a footpath sign on the right near the cricket club. Go through the kissing gate and follow the path to another kissing gate. Go through it and then turn left and to another kissing gate. Go through it and out into the road and right past the entrance to the Cadbury's factory entrance and to a small roundabout.

Go straight ahead and over a railway bridge with Chirk station below you on the right. Go past the entrance to an industrial estate on the right and continue until you reach a footpath sign on the right. Follow it through the trees and then you will see steps on your left. Go up them and follow the path

The impressive gates of Chirk Castle

until you see a kissing gate to the left. Go through it and then straight up the field to a kissing gate. Go through it and out to the road. To your left are the impressive gates to Chirk Castle. You can either visit them now (it'll only take a few minutes) or when you leave the Castle.

From the stile go to the right and follow the road until you come to a public footpath sign pointing to the left. You can only follow this path between 1 April and 30 September. During the rest of the year you will have to continue along the road to the entrance and then up the road to the Castle car park.

If you are following the path, go to the left through the kissing gate and up field aiming for the left of trees on the right hand side and to a stile. Go over the stile and straight ahead to a kissing gate and a white-topped pole. Go through the gate and up the left hand side of the field to another kissing gate and white-topped pole. Go through the gate and straight ahead up the field and when you see the Castle on your left there is a

stile in front of you. Go over it, to the left and up the lane back
to the Castle car park.

OTHER POINTS OF INTEREST

Chirk. This border town stands on the escarpment above the
point at which the rivers Ceiriog and Dee meet. The name Chirk
is thought to be an English corruption of Ceiriog, whilst its
Welsh name Y Waun means 'the moor'. Due to Chirk's strategic
position a motte and bailey castle was built here by the
Normans in the early 12th century. In the 19th century, vital
road, rail and canal links were developed and Chirk became a
staging post on the London to Holyhead mail road, with
passengers breaking their journey at a coaching inn in the town.
St Mary's Church, which has records dating back to 1163,
occupies a central position in the town and contains monuments
to the Trevors and the Myddletons, both local families of note.

Offa's Dyke. Offa was King of Mercia from 757 to 796 AD. His
kingdom covered the area between the Trent/Mersey rivers in
the north to the Thames Valley in the south, and from the Welsh
border in the west to the Fens in the east. Offa's Dyke is a linear
earthwork which roughly follows the Welsh/English boundary.
It consists of a ditch and rampart with the ditch on the Welsh-
facing side, and appears to have been carefully aligned to
present an open view into Wales from along its length.
Originally it was about thirty yards (27m) wide and nine yards
(8m) from the ditch bottom to the bank top. The dyke appears to
have been constructed in response to events in the border
region, but whether it was intended as an agreed boundary, as a
defensive structure with long lost additional fortifications or for
some other use is not known. It is thought to have been started
in about 785 AD and to have taken several years to build. Much
of the dyke is still traceable along the eighty miles. In places it
still retains most of its original dimensions while in other parts
it has disappeared due to 1200 years of farming activity and its
presence can only be detected by archaeological work.

Shropshire Union Canal. It runs for about sixty miles in all. It is not one single waterway but an amalgamation of half a dozen separate companies in 1846. The Llangollen branch, which reached Chirk in 1801, is perhaps Britain's most popular cruising canal and Chirk Marina is well situated between Thomas Telford's two magnificent aqueducts at Chirk and at Pontcysyllte. It is possible to walk across both aqueducts if you have a head for heights. Chirk Aqueduct built between 1796 and 1801 by Telford and William Jessop is 70 feet (22m) high with 10 arches. At the northern end of the aqueduct, the canal enters Darkie Tunnel which is wide enough for a single barge and walkway. It is possible to walk through the quarter mile long tunnel using the walkway.

Telford's aqueduct at Pontcysyllte.

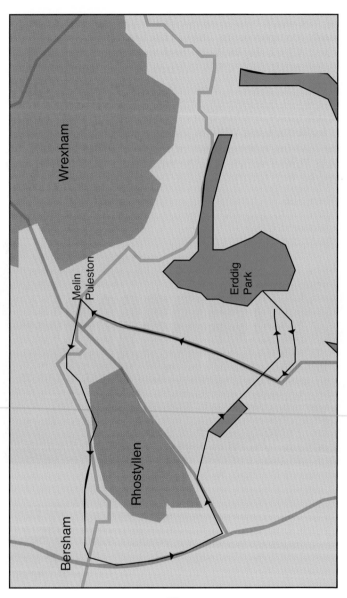

Wrexham

Erddig
Park

Melin
Puleston

Rhostyllen

Bersham

2. ERDDİG
Tel. 01938 557019

Erddig

The mansion was designed in 1687 by Thomas Webb for Joshua Edisbury, the high sheriff of Denbighshire. In 1718 the buildings were sold to John Mellor (1665-1733), master of the chancellery, who enlarged and furnished it. When he died, the property passed to his nephew Simon Yorke and it remained in the Yorke family until it was given to the National Trust in 1973. The family was rather unconventional, with Philip Yorke being a vegetarian since he was five years

Dovecote at Erddig

old. The family members had an interest in antiquity and were archivists hoarding everything, no matter how trivial. The family kept the house as it was during the 18th century and did not install electricity, gas or mains water until well into the 20th century.

The stunning state rooms display most of their original 18th and 19th century furniture and furnishings, including some exquisite Chinese wallpaper. It has an extensive range of outbuildings, including a kitchen, laundry, bakehouse, stables, sawmill, smithy and joiner's shop. The large walled garden has been restored to its 18th century formal design and has a Victorian ornamental flower beds and yew walk. It also contains the National Collection of Ivy.

The walk – *from Erddig to Felin Puleston, and then along part of the Clywedog Valley Trail to the Bersham Heritage Centre and back to Erddig.* 4 miles – 2.5 hours (not including visit to Iron Works and Nant Mill)

Felin Pulestone

Park your car in the Erddig car park. The walled car park closes at six o'clock and the main gates at seven – so don't leave it too late! There is no bus service to Erddig but you can get a bus to Rhostyllen and start the walk from **Felin Puleston.** Go out of the Erddig car park and down the lane. You will see signs pointing to 'Chester' and 'Whitchurch'; follow the lane to Chester. Go down the lane towards the Erddig entrance and then keep right along Hafod Road, ignoring the paths on both sides of the road. You will go past Manor Farm on the left and you then go down to a junction where you will see a sign for Felin Puleston on the right. Follow it, but before you go into the car park, you will see a path going up to the left between two trees. This is the **Clywedog Valley Trail.**

Go up the path, then down, under the road bridge under the railway bridge, over a footbridge, past red-bricked houses on the right, past a bench and then left towards some railings and onto another path. Go left, over a footbridge and to a stile on your right. Go over the stile and straight ahead along the left

Bersham Heritage Centre

hand side of the field and you will return to the river Clywedog and to a stile. Go over it and follow the path through the trees, past a house on the left and to a stile. Go over it into a lane to the right and over a bridge and to another stile near a cattle grid.

Carry on along the lane between some houses and past the **Black Lion Inn** on the right. Go straight ahead along the hedge and past a weir on your left. Go to the right and up the steps into a playing field. Turn to the right and up the steps and to the main road. Go to the left and along the pavement to the **Bersham Heritage Centre.** You are now about half way, so why not have a rest either at the Centre or at the Black Lion?

Having visited the Centre, continue along the pavement to a junction. You can either go straight ahead to visit the **Iron Works** which is about a quarter of a mile away and **Nant Mill** which is a mile and a half away and return to this junction, or go left and return to Erddig.

From the junction, go left, following the Erddig sign over the bridge and up the hill. Go past Wilkinson Drive and a football field on the left and to a junction. Turn left into Rhostyllen. Go past the Parish Hall and Institute on the left and to a junction. Keep to the right, past Liver Cottages on the right and continue

along the road to a junction. There is an old coal tip on your right. Cross the road and on your left you will see a public footpath sign and a stile in the hedge. Go over the stile and go left following the broad path past the cemetery and down towards the railway.

Go over a stile, cross the railway carefully and over another stile to a field. Go straight ahead with the hedge on your right to a stile. Go over it and to a stile near a tree to your left. Go

Nant Mill

26

over it and into Hafod Road and to another stile straight in front of you. Cross the road and go over a stile and then right to a footbridge. Cross this and then go up the field with a farmhouse on your right and to a gate. Go through it and then left and up the lane back to the Erddig car park.

OTHER POINTS OF INTEREST
Bersham Heritage Centre. This building was originally a school, built on the site of an old ironworks. It contains information on 300 years of iron and steelmaking at Bersham and nearby Brymbo. You can see local artist blacksmiths at work here and visit the Victorian schoolroom. The structure outside the centre is a reconstructed horse whimsey, a replica of one used at Llwyneinion mine for winding men and ore up and down the shafts.

Bersham Iron Works. Ironmaking started in the Clywedog Valley as early as the 17th century, and it was in the 18th century, when the ironworks was extended by Issac and then John Wilkinson, that Bersham acquired an international reputation. It was here that John Wilkinson used his revolutionary process to bore cannon and cylinders from solid cast metal. Cannon from Bersham were used in the American War of Independence and in many of Britain's foreign campaigns, while Wilkinson's cylinders enabled Boulton and Watt's steam engines to power the Industrial Revolution. At the ironworks can be seen excavated remains of the first blast furnace in Wales to smelt iron with coke, an 18th century wagonway used to transport raw material to the works and tools and personal items found during archaeological excavation.

Black Lion Inn. It is known locally as the Hole in the Wall, due to the workers of nearby Bersham ironworks having made a shortcut to get to the pub.

Clywedog Valley Trail. During the 18th century this valley was a hive of industrial activity, with 17 mills along its length – fulling mills to prepare cloth, mills for grinding corn and malt, and paper mills. Huge waterwheels powered the bellows blasting air into the iron furnaces at Bersham, and to drive winding and pumping machinery in the lead mines. The trail starts from the Minera Lead Mines, past Nant Mill, through Plas Power Woods to Bersham Ironworks and Bersham Heritage Centre and to Felin Puleston.

Felin Puleston. It is now an educational centre, but at one time the buildings were one of Erddig's tenanted farms. Felin Puleston or mill was built in the 16th century, but in 1769 it was converted for farm use.

Nant Mill. There has been a mill here for hundreds of years. The original mill was probably for fulling (thickening woven woollen cloth), but by the late 18th century it was a corn mill. It briefly reopened during the second world war. The old mill these days is the home to bats. The Lesser Horseshoe Bats use the tunnel under the road that drained water from the wheelpit into the river and Pipistrelle Bats roost in the roof.

Nant Mill

Bersham Heritage Centre

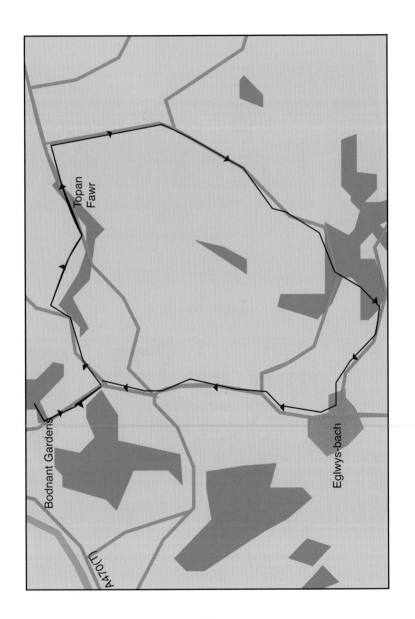

3. Bodnant Gardens
Tel. 01492 650460

Part of the nurseries at Bodnant Gardens

It has probably the most spectacular gardens in the world. It is situated above the river Conwy and has stunning views across Snowdonia. Begun in 1875, Bodnant is the creation of four generations of the Aberconway family and the gardens feature huge Italianate terraces and formal lawns on its upper level, with a wooded valley, stream and wild garden below. There are dramatic colours throughout the season, with fine collections of rhododendrons, magnolias and camellias and a spectacular laburnum arch 55 yards long.

The walk – *from Bodnant Gardens uphill along winding rural roads and footpaths and down to Eglwys-bach and back to Bodnant Gardens.* 4.5 miles – 2.25 hours

The family manor at Bodnant Gardens

Park your car in the Gardens' car park (there is a bus stop near the entrance). Go out of the car park, turn left up the hill and then down and then along Ffordd Bodnant Uchaf. When you come to a junction, keep left and up almost to the top of the hill. After you pass a house on your left you will see a lane on the right. Although there is no public footpath sign here there is a right of way. Go along the lane past Ty'n y Coed and then right and through four gates.

Go straight ahead – don't turn left. Go through another gate and another one and out to a road. Go left and up the hill past Topan Fawr on the left to a junction and straight ahead to another junction. Go straight ahead again and then to the right. Go to the top of the hill and to a junction. Turn right in the direction of Eglwys-bach.

Ignore the public footpath on the right and go past a ruin on your left. Cross a small bridge, up the hill and then down and look for a public footpath sign and stile on the left. Go over the

The Bee Inn, Eglwys-bach

Eglwys-bach

Bodnant Gardens

stile and along the path through the trees – be careful here as the path is narrow and there is a drop to the stream below. Go over the stream near the bridge and up the path through the wooded glade to a stile.

Go over the stile and up to a track and before reaching the agricultural building you will see a stile on your left. Go over it and over another one and then go right past a house on the right and down the track. Go over the footbridge and then up and then down past a house on the right. Go over the bridge and up to the road. Go to your right and down the hill. Ignore the two public footpaths either side of the road near Bwlch Glas and go down the hill to Eglwys-bach.

At the junction, turn right, past the Bee Inn – which dates back to 1876 – on the right and a plaque to **Owen Williams** on the house on the left. Pass **St Martin's Church** on the left and along the road through Brymbo and Graig and up a small hill to a telephone kiosk.

The Italian terraces, Bodnant Gardens

Keep straight ahead in the direction of Bodnant. Ignore the two roads on your right and go straight ahead and back to the Bodnant Gardens' car park.

OTHER POINTS OF INTEREST
Owen Williams (1877-1956). Owen Williams was a shoemaker who used to get up at five o'clock every morning to practise the piano. He wrote a number of well-known hymn tunes.
St Martin's Church. The church was mentioned in the Norwich Taxation of 1254. It was rebuilt in 1782, and restored in 1882.

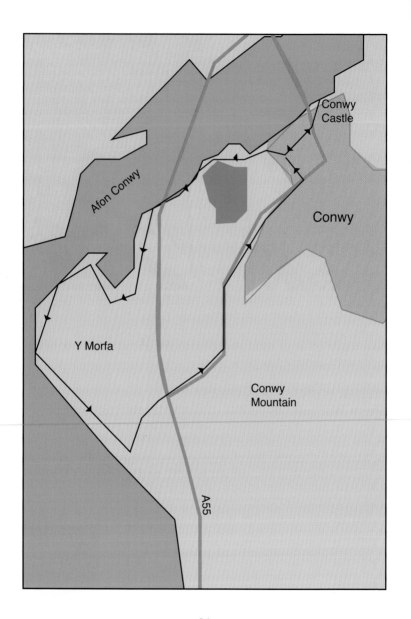

Conwy
Castle

Afon Conwy

Conwy

Y Morfa

Conwy
Mountain

A55

4. Conwy Suspension Bridge and Aberconwy House

Tel. 01492 592246

Conwy Suspension Bridge

The Telford road bridge was opened in 1826 – built by Thomas Telford who had earlier, in 1819, built the Menai Suspension Bridge. It took three years to build an embankment from the eastern side, to an island in the middle of the river. The rest of the river was crossed by the bridge. The towers of the bridge were built to blend in with the castle walls and towers. It is said that at one time midgets used to collect the tolls to cross the bridge as the house is so small. The story is that a travelling circus stayed in Conwy in the 1930s but went bankrupt, stranding the troupe in the town. A number of the midgets decided to stay there.

Aberconwy House escaped the destruction of the town

Aberconwy House

Conwy Castle

during Glyndŵr's rebellion and is the best surviving example of a medieval town house in northern Wales. It is mainly of 14th century construction and appears to have been built using techniques commonly employed in south-eastern England. As the town was populated by the English at that time, this is not surprising. It was probably the home of a prosperous merchant, with the basement – as now – a shop, although at that time the road level outside was about three feet lower than at present. The first floor contained the main living room and a separate kitchen. The top floor was open to the roof and was used as the sleeping quarters.

The walk – *from the centre of Conwy to the castle and suspension bridge, past Aberconwy House, down to the quay and along Marine Drive and the shore at Conwy Morfa and back into Conwy.*
4.5 miles – 2 hours

The quay at Conwy

Park in Conwy, there are two car parks in the centre of the town and another on the western side at Bodlondeb. Walk towards the **castle** and then along the suspension bridge. At the eastern end there is a small toll house where you pay your fee. Return along the bridge and into the centre of town. Walk along Castle Street and you will see Aberconwy House on the left hand corner.

After visiting it, cross the road using the crossing and go down to the quay. Turn left, go past the **smallest house in Britain** and under the arch into Marine Walk. Continue along the shore until you reach the road. Turn right, over a bridge and along Morfa Drive.

Continue along Morfa Drive and over the bridge that crosses the A55 Expressway to a T-junction, turn left and along Ellis Way to a mini-roundabout. Turn right down Meirion Drive to the water's edge. Here there is a shelter with a plaque commemorating the building of the **Mulberry Harbour.**

Go left along the water's edge, then turn right. Walk along the pavement and then follow the footpath to where the ferry Terminal used to be. Opposite the river is **Deganwy.** Follow the path along the water's edge to your left. In the car park on your left is an information board with photographs of the Morfa, its history and wildlife and the building of the tunnel under the river. Return to the path that runs alongside the shore. On your left is Conwy Golf Club.

Continue along the shore to where Pearl Kitchens used to be. You will then leave the estuary and follow the sea shore. On your left, on the edge of the golf course, are two concrete structures. These were used for target practice at the Firing Range. The area to your left is Conwy Morfa. When you come to the road, bear left, although it is worth first going a few yards to the right to see the information board on the wildlife of the Morfa. Otherwise go left along the pavement, past the Aberconwy Park entrance. Bear right, go over the bridge that crosses the A55 Expressway and then over the railway bridge.

Carry on along the pavement. On your right you will see a path going up **Conwy Mountain.**

Proceed along the pavement and under the railway bridge. On your left, on a corner, is a white cottage with a large chimney in the centre of the roof. This is a former **tollhouse**. You will then reach the entrance to Bodlondeb, where you may have parked your car or proceed into the town to one of the other two car parks.

OTHER POINTS OF INTEREST

Castle. It was designed by Edward I's master castle builder James of St George, who was summoned from Europe to implement Edward's plans. It is one of the key fortresses in his attempt to secure his invasion, establish a colony and to supress the Welsh. Building started in 1283 (the year following Llywelyn ein Llyw Olaf's death) and was completed four years later using 1,500 workmen conscripted from almost every county in England. They were often under armed guard to prevent them from escaping.

The castle has a distinctive elongated shape with two barbicans, eight massive towers and a great bow-shaped hall. The towers originally had conical roofs. The walls were coated in limewash and could be seen for miles. The stone used for the construction of the castle and walls is Silurian grit. Pinkish sandstone from across the river was used to form the windows, door-jambs, arrow loops, chimneys etc, while sandstone from Chester was used to construct the roof arches. Timber was brought down river from Trefriw and beyond, and the lead and coal for the forges came by sea from near Flint. The cost of building was nearly £15,000. For many years the castle was not properly maintained and it was bought by Viscount Conwy in 1628 for just £100. The local authority took it over in the 19th century. It is now cared for by Cadw (Welsh Historic Monuments).

Conwy Mountain. Here are stone circles and the remains of the

Castell Deganwy

hill fort of Caer Lleon, built most probably to guard the crossing point on the Conwy. On the north side, the hill is so steep that the fort needed no additional, manmade defence. Towards the south-west, there is a simple gap which formed the original entrance. Today you can still see the remains of about 50 stone huts and levelled house platforms. To the south, the huts were located within a thick stone wall. The citadel was originally constructed on the rocky summit of the ridge and was defended by an earthen rampart and ditch. Excavations at the site have found slingstones, querns, stone pestles and mortars but no datable remains.

Llywelyn Fawr

Deganwy. The twin hills above the

42

The Smallest House in Britain

modern village of Deganwy housed a fortress that was in use from at least the Roman era until its final destruction in 1277. Hardly anything now remains of the castle. In the 6th century, Deganwy was the *llys* (fortified court) of Maelgwn, Lord of Anglesey, who died in 547 AD. In 1080, Robert of Rhuddlan built the first Norman castle on the site, but he was later killed by Welsh pirates near Great Orme. In the early 13th century it was occupied by Llywelyn Fawr who built a stone castle here. After Llywelyn's death Henry III began to rebuild it. A letter sent from Deganwy during Henry's 1254 campaign tells vividly of the hardships and lack of food in the castle. Prisoners were slaughtered on both sides and the heads of Welshmen were brought back to the castle as trophies after each successful sortie. In 1263, Prince Edward, later to be king, had been able to restock his castle with the help of his mercenaries but the Welsh starved the garrison out by cutting off his supply chain later in the year. Llywelyn ap Gruffudd then made it so thoroughly

The Telford bridge tollhouse

indefensible that it was never raised again. Edward I decided to build a new castle across the river on a prominent rock, where it could be supplied by sea via a fortified dock. Local tradition has it that the stone of Deganwy Castle was reused in the making of Conwy Castle and its town walls.

Mulberry Harbour. During the Second World War, floating harbours which played a vital part in the D-Day landings were prefabricated here. The project was supposed to be top secret, but with 900 men working here it was very difficult to keep it quiet. The men arrived in 1943 and lived in huts on the Morfa. Work went on 24 hours a day with powerful arc lights in use at night. Some of the larger structures, the Phoenix Caissons, weighed 6,000 tons and measured 20 feet (6m) square by 60 feet (18.5m) high. The construction site occupied ten acres and was situated on land at the far side of the present marina. The modern pub to your right has been named the Mulberry Inn after the harbour.

Smallest house in Britain. It is widely believed that between the end of the row of cottages was a very small gap between that and another row of cottages which was demolished during the 20th century. The house was built in the gap between the two rows. The last person to live there was reputed to be well over six feet tall.

Tollhouse. It was erected in 1825 to serve the Holyhead route built by the Caernarvonshire Turnpike Trust which was founded in 1768. The standard toll was six pence per horse and a carriage with four horses had to pay two shillings. In 1882, local councils took over road maintenance and tolls were abolished.

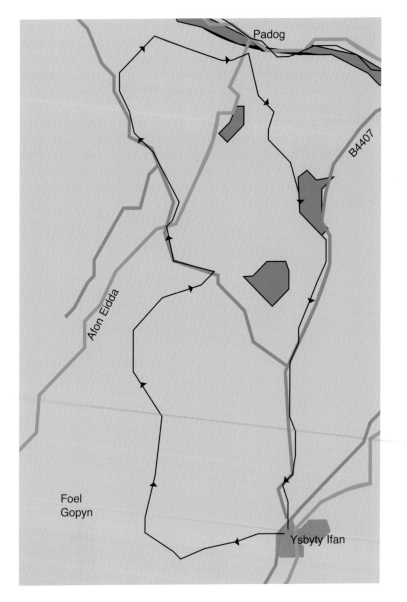

Padog

B4407

Afon Eidda

Foel
Gopyn

Ysbyty Ifan

5. YSBYTY IFAN
Tel. no. of mill: 01690 790333

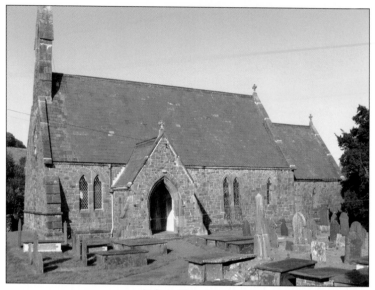

Ysbyty Ifan church

In 1856, Lord Penrhyn, owner of the Penrhyn quarries who lived at Penrhyn Castle (see walk 10), bought the Ysbyty Estate which had over thirty farms, from the then owners Sir Edward Pryce Lloyd and Edward Mostyn Lloyd. The estate provided substantial rents for Lord Penrhyn as records show. For example, the widow of a Robert Hughes who rented the mill and the meadow in 1870 paid a rent of £27.10.00 per year. The rent collected

The old mill wheel

Old mill at Ysbyty Ifan, now occupied by Cwlwm.

from the whole village – a total of about a hundred farms and homes – was £1,703.13.00, which was a considerable sum for those days.

The National Trust owns and manages the 52 farms which are on the estate today, as well as the old mill.

The walk – *from the old mill to Foel Gopyn and then along winding roads, tracks and footpaths to Padog and back to Ysbyty Ifan.*
5.5 miles – 3 hours

There is space for about half a dozen cars to park near the **old mill** at **Ysbyty Ifan** now occupied by **Cwlwm** which produces a full wedding service from cakes and dresses to stationery and harp music. Why not have a look around and have a bite to eat at the **Popty Pen Uchaf** cafe? There is an infrequent bus service to Ysbyty Ifan. You should ring Traveline Cymru (0870 6082608) if you intend travelling there by bus. Turn left out of the mill and then right at the next turning past the old almshouses (see plaque on the gable end).

Go up the hill; don't turn right into the farm but keep straight up along the rough track to a gate. Go through it and proceed along the track to another gate. Go through it and up the track to a lane. Turn right and go along the lane to the crest of the hill and then down.

Ignore the lane on the left going to Foel Gopyn and the footpath sign on the right and go straight ahead along the road. Then, look for a public footpath sign on a post on your left but pointing to the right; go to the right to a public footpath sign and a small gate. Go through it and walk with the fence on your right. Ignore a stile on your right and go straight ahead along the fence to the gate. At the time of writing it was not possible to open the gate, so climb over it and carry on down the slope and through a gap in a wall and to a lane with a gate on the right.

Go through the gate and along the lane to another gate and through the farmyard and then right through a gate, up the lane and to the left, over a bridge and through two gates. Ignore the turning to the right and continue down the hill. Also ignore the stile near the cowshed and go right and up the hill towards Tŷ Mawr. Go through two gates and to a lane.

Turn left and down the hill and over the bridge that crosses afon Eidda. Ignore the stile on the left and go up the hill, ignoring a lane to the right and the lane to Fron Ddu and then go through the gate towards Bryn Bras. Go along the lane, through a gate, through the farmyard and to the right and along the track through two gates. Cross the stream and down to a gate. Don't go through this gate but go left along the fence to a small gate. Go through it, along the path through the trees, over the footbridge and out near the **A5** close to a telephone kiosk at Padog.

Go to the right to a large expanse of tarmac. To the right is Capel Padog. Follow the path between the garage and the house to a gate. Go through it and up along the wall to a kissing gate and then straight up aiming for two trees and an old wall. Continue up the slope aiming for a farm. When you reach the fence go to the left and you will reach a stile. Go over it and go to the right towards the farm. You will then reach a footpath sign and a stile. At the time of writing the stile was broken but it is possible to go to the field through a gate to the right.

Go up the field with a forest on your left and to a stile. Go over it and when you have gone past the trees you will see a stile on your left. Go over it and over a small stream and to the right and to a track. Go left to the top of the hill and to a junction. Keep straight ahead to the top of the hill and through a gate and to another junction. Go straight ahead and down the hill and back to Ysbyty Ifan.

OTHER POINTS OF INTEREST

A5. Built by Thomas Telford, after pressure to improve the mail service between London and Dublin, work started on this route in 1815. Up until the 1990s it was the main route into northern Wales, connecting with the ferry service to Ireland in Holyhead. The road starts from the Marble Arch in London and then follows the old Roman road (Watling Street) to the Welsh border, marked by a bridge over the river Dee. After winding its way through Snowdonia, it crosses the Menai Strait and proceeds along Anglesey to the ferry terminal at Holyhead. The A5 has now been given the status of a Historic Route

Cwlwm. In the old mill, six local farming wives, all with experience in their different fields, under the name of Cwlwm, offer various services for wedding ceremonies and breakfasts – all under the same roof.

Popty Pen Uchaf. The bakery and tea room is a venture by one of the tenants of the National Trust's upland farms. Popty Pen Uchaf is part of Cwlwm wedding services, and makes the wedding cakes. Only the best ingredients are used in the traditional recipes and seasonal products that are on sale.

The Old Mill. The mill, which was built around 1800, served the neighbouring farms and was an integral part of the village. It is likely that the mill was established on the recommendation of Lord Penrhyn who had the legal right to insist that all the corn grown by his tenants should be ground in his mill. The influence of local mills such as this one in Ysbyty Ifan declined in the early twentieth century with the growth of larger companies in urban areas. By 1940, the last miller, Thomas John Roberts, had started supplementing his income by using the mill to generate electricity for the village. But it was not sufficient for the needs of all the village, and the further from the mill the lower the power. The mill closed around 1960 and in 1997 it became a listed building. The old water wheel is still behind the mill as well as some of the old machinery inside.

Ysbyty Ifan. The original name of the village was Dolgynwal, but it changed when a hospice and garrison was established here in 1190. The *ysbyty* or hospice was established by Hospice Knights, later better known as the Knights of St John of Jerusalem. It became a refuge for travellers and received support from wealthy local landowners and the village grew around it as well as becoming a rich agricultural area. There is a plaque on the present church which is on the site of the old hospice. The knights were given certain exemptions and immunities from the law, so that no officer of the crown could enter their property to arrest lawbreakers. It is said that the immunity was never repealed and the hospice became a refuge

for bandits who terrorised the neighbourhood at the end of the Middle Ages.

Ysbyty Ifan

51

6. Tŷ Mawr Wybrnant
Tel. 01690 760213

Tŷ Mawr Wybrnant

Tŷ Mawr Wybrnant is situated in the Wybrnant valley near Penmachno and was the birthplace of Bishop William Morgan, the translator of the Bible into Welsh. The house has been restored to its probable 16th/17th century appearance and includes a display of Welsh Bibles and Bibles in other languages and an exhibition room. In the house behind Tŷ Mawr is an exhibition on the drovers.

The walk – *from y Wybrant, over the mountain to Dolwyddelan following a possible old **drovers'** route and then back along the banks of afon Lledr and through the forest to Wybrant.*
7 miles – 3.45 hours

You can reach Wybrnant either from Penmachno or from the

The 'William Morgan' Welsh bible at Tŷ Mawr Wybrnant

road between Betws-y-coed and Dolwyddelan after passing Fairy Glen. Park your car outside Tŷ Mawr – there is space for about half a dozen cars there or in a small car park further up. There is no bus service here, but you could go by bus to **Dolwyddelan** and begin your journey from there through the forest to Wybrnant and back over the mountain to Dolwyddelan.

Go towards the house called Pwll y Gath (to the right of Tŷ Mawr) and you will see a sign on a post. Follow it to a gate. Go through it and to the left, walking with the wall. Follow the track between two walls to a gate and stile. Go over it and then up the path that goes alongside the wall to a lane. Cross the lane and go straight ahead in the direction of the Dolwyddelan sign. Follow the path alongside the wall to another lane. Cross it and go straight ahead along the path. It can be a bit wet here after heavy rain as with other parts of the path further along.

Go through the trees to a stile. Go over it and to the top of the hill. Follow the path along the flat moorland to a post in the ground and along the path with a large rock on the right. Continue towards another large rock with Foel Felan mountain on your right and keep left and then down towards a stile. Go over it and along the path through the trees to an old gate (you will have to climb over it) and out of the trees.

Go down the field to an old fence where once there was a gate. Go over the fence and then down between the trees and a fence and through the trees to a gate. Go through it, down and then turn right to another gate. Go through it and out to a lane. Go left. The village of Dolwyddelan is in front of you.

Go past an old quarry on your left to a gate and stile. Go over the stile and continue along the lane to a fence, gate and stile. Go over the stile, past some houses on the left and to the right and to some bridges. Go over the railway bridge. Turn right and not into Dolwyddelan, but if you have the time why not pop into the village? There are two hotels and a shop there.

Go to the right past a school and further along Tŷ Isaf farm and to a gate. Go through it and walk along the banks of **Afon Lledr**. Don't go left over the bridge but keep straight ahead to a gate. Go through it and straight ahead along the wall, past a house on the right to a post in the field and straight ahead until you see a small tunnel on the right. Go through it under the railway and to the left to a stile

Cross the stile and up through the trees, along the side of the field and then down through the trees to a gate and smaller gate. Go through the smaller gate and past a house on the left and you will see a stile on the right. Go over it and up the field with a stream to your right until you come to a gate. Go through the gate to a lane. Keep left and up the lane, past an agricultural building on the right and then down to a gate and stile. Go over the stile and continue along the lane, ignoring a path that comes up from the left. You will then see a path going to the right. Follow it through the trees, past a post with an arrow on it near a ruin and then straight ahead to a post that points right, up a very rough track and follow it to the left.

You will then reach a post with an arrow pointing to the right, follow it up a steep slope to a post with its arrow pointing upwards. Go through the trees, past four posts to a piece of level ground. Go past another post and through a gap in a wall to a stile and arrow. Go over the stile and keep straight ahead. There is no path now and you will have to walk through long, wiry grass, heather and bilberry bushes. Go straight ahead with a pine forest on your right (keep within about a hundred yards of the forest).

When you see a deciduous forest in front of you, you will come across a path. Follow it to the left, following a fence until you reach a gate. Go through it and into a field. Go to the right and you will find a gap behind a rock. Go through it and down the field along a poor track and to a bit of path that runs alongside a fence to a gate. Go through it and down through the trees to a small gate. Go through it and past Tan y Clogwyn to a lane. Go to the right and back to Tŷ Mawr.

Bishop William Morgan
A gifted scholar, he studied Hebrew, Greek and Latin at Cambridge University. He was priest of several northern parishes before becoming Bishop of Llandaff and later St Asaph. His greatest contribution was his great work in translating the Bible into Welsh, which he did at the behest of Elizabeth I. He finished the work in 1588 and from then on the Welsh could read the scriptures in their own language. This, say many, is what saved the Welsh language from extinction. The New Testament had already been translated into Welsh by William

St Gwyddelan church

Salesbury in 1567, but Bishop Morgan's Bible gave the language a formal orthography and a standard written Welsh. His wide vocabulary and the poetry of the translation gave the Welsh a dignified language. Every Sunday, with the royal seal of approval, the Welsh people would hear this dignified language from the pulpits and this was a great contribution to the survival of the language.

OTHER POINTS OF INTEREST

Afon Lledr. It is a tributary of the Conwy, rising on Moel Siabod and joining the main river just outside Betws-y-coed. It is noted for its salmon and trout fishing.

Dolwyddelan. Legend has it that a young woman called Elan, famed for her looks, wished her name and reputation to live forever. She declared: "Not for nothing am I able to immortalise my name. If there is not any other land prettier than this, henceforth my name shall be upon it." But the name of the

Dolwyddelan castle

village most probably came from St Gwyddelan, who founded a church here in the sixth century. The present church is reputed to have been built by Maredudd ap Ieuan ap Robert, a distant descendant of Llywelyn Fawr (the Great), who came to live here in the 1500s. Maredudd died in 1525 and is buried in the church, and there is a memorial to him and his family on the north wall of the church.

Dolwyddelan castle. It is the birthplace of Llywelyn ap Iorwerth (Llywelyn Fawr). The earliest buildings are early 13th century. The castle covers two routes into Snowdonia, and it remained an important stronghold for his grandson, Llywelyn ap Gruffudd, but its capture by the English – perhaps through treachery – in 1283 was a turning point in the English campaign. It was immediately repaired and garrisoned by Edward I. The English maintained a military presence here until 1290, but their long-term strategy of control relied on military and administrative centres accessible by sea, and inland castles became increasingly irrelevant. The castle was occupied again in the 15th century, when it was leased to Maredudd ap Ieuan, who added an upper storey to the keep.

Drovers. The export of store cattle from Wales to the rich pasturelands of England played a vital part in the Welsh economy from the mid-13th century onwards and by the mid-17th century cattle exports were one of the primary sources of Welsh revenue. The growth of urban populations during the late 18th century led to an increased demand for beef and thousands of Welsh cattle were driven into England for fattening after being purchased by dealers and drovers at local fairs. In 1794, 10,000 cattle were exported from Anglesey and by 1810 14,000 were being sent annually to the Midlands from Anglesey and the Llŷn Peninsula alone. Gentlemen employed drovers as carriers of money and news, and Welsh drovers pioneered the establishment of banks in west Wales.

The Welsh drovers who took cattle to London were regarded by the townspeople with suspicion. An account of Barnet Fair in *Farmers Magazine* in 1856 refers in a rather uncomplimentary fashion to the Welsh drovers: "Imagine some hundreds of bullocks like an immense forest of horns, propelled hurriedly towards you amid the hideous and uproarious shouting of a set of semi-barbarous drovers ... driving their mad and noisy herds over every person they meet if not fortunate enough to get out of their way ... the noisy 'hurrahs' of lots of 'un-English speaking' Welshmen ... to be seen throwing up their long-worn, shapeless hats high in the air ... uttering at the same time a ... gibberish which no-one can understand but themselves."

The size of a drove of cattle varied according to the time of year and demand, ranging from one hundred to four hundred cattle attended by four to eight drovers and their dogs. It took three to four days for the drove to settle down to a steady two miles per hour, a pace which would give the animals opportunity to graze by the wayside. They would cover between fifteen and twenty miles per day so as not to force the cattle and and cause them to lose condition. A long and strenuous day over rough mountain track would be followed by a shorter day's travelling to give the cattle an opportunity to recuperate. The dealer or the foreman drover would ride ahead to arrange accommodation for both men and animals, at either farms or inns, many possessing paddocks where cattle could be held overnight.

The end came with the extension of the railway to Shrewsbury in 1856 and cattle being loaded into railway trucks for the remainder of the journey. Within a few years the railways had reached into Wales enabling the cattle to be carried all the way to the markets.

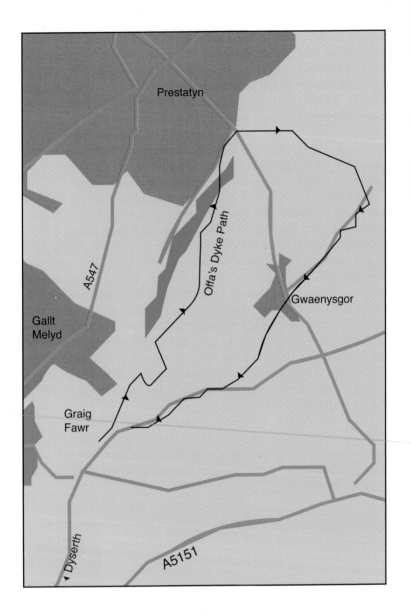

Prestatyn

Offa's Dyke Path

A547

Gallt
Melyd

Gwaenysgor

Graig
Fawr

Dyserth

A5151

7. Graig Fawr, Dyserth

Graig Fawr

The exposed location near the coast and the bleak limestone outcrops have resulted in the presence of a number of species normally associated with sea cliffs. Graig Fawr is also a complex archaeological site with much use in many periods including metal ore mining. The hill, which is about 61 acres in area, was given to the National Trust in 1973 by Sir Geoffrey Summers of the John Summers Steelworks at Shotton, north-eastern Wales. The land is let to a local farmer to graze sheep, and grazing is important to support the wild flowers that are on the land.

The walk – *from Graig Fawr along Offa's Dyke Path with its spectacular views of the northern coast of Wales and back through Gwaunysgor to Graig Fawr.*
5 miles – 2.5 hours with another 20 minutes to visit the top of Graig Fawr and back

Start the walk from the Graig Fawr car park. There is no bus service therefore you would have to walk up the steep hill from **Dyserth**. Go out of the car park and to the left. (To your right, on private land, are the remains of **Dyserth Castle**.) Go to the junction and left up the hill, then down and up and you will see a public footpath sign on your left; this is the **Offa's Dyke Path**. Follow the path through the gate along the track to a red-roofed house. Go to the right through a kissing gate and follow the path up and then down to another kissing gate.

Go through it and past an old quarry on your left. Ignore the path to the left and go straight up to a junction with signs. Turn to the left. Ignore the small gate on the right and go straight ahead with the fence. Go up to the public footpath signs and to the right towards **Prestatyn** and past the remains of **Pant y Fachwen** cottage. Go up the steep path and then down past an old mine shaft on the left and up through the bushes to a public footpath sign and stile.

Don't go over the stile but straight up and then down, over a flight of steps and continue down until you reach a road. Turn right, up a steep hill, around the bend to the right and past a water treatment works on the right and you will see a public footpath sign on the left.

Follow the path through the trees to a stile. Go over it and follow the path to the left to another stile. Go over it and up the edge of the field to another stile. Go over it and to yet another stile. Go over it and up the field with the masts on your right to another stile. Go over it and then straight ahead across the field. (If there are crops in the field, go to the right following the edge of the field.) You will then reach a gate on the right. Go through it to a track and then left and you will reach a junction. Go to the right along the track, past a bench and down the tarmaced lane.

Ignore the footpath to the right and continue to **Gwaunysgor.** You will reach a junction – go to the left. There are now three roads going to the right. The first goes to the **Eagle and Child Inn** – an excellent place for a break. Now either go

Eagle and Child Inn, Gwaenysgor

along the second road and through the churchyard of the
Church of St Mary Magdalen and then to the right, or along the
third road past the church.

Go down the track and when you have gone past the last
house you will see a stile on the left. Go over it and along the
path to a gate and stile. Go over the stile and along to a gate and
a stone stile. Go over the stile and follow the path to the right to
another stile. Go over it and left and along the track to a gate. Go
through it and out into the road. Ignore the public footpaths on
the right and left and go down the hill to a junction. Turn right
and return to the car park.

OTHER POINTS OF INTEREST
Church of St Mary Magdalen. The church is recorded in the
Doomsday Book, but it is unlikely that the present single-
chambered building goes back to that time. Its core, however, is
certainly medieval, perhaps even Norman, and it has been

Church of St Magdalen, Gwaenysgor

suggested that it was enlarged during the 15th century. It has a 13th century font and a curious wooden entrance arch displaying Christian symbols. The building is aligned almost due east to west. The stone slabbed floor includes two large gravestones at the west end, one of 1711 the other of 1743. A small bronze figure of a saddled horse, perhaps Romano-British, was found during the excavation of a grave, and a Roman milestone was discovered built into the churchyard wall; it is now in the National Museum of Wales. The small polygonal churchyard includes a sundial pillar of 1663 and several 17th century graves.

Dyserth. The village nestles against the slope of Moel Hiraddug, on which there is an Iron Age hill fort, difficult to explore because of the quarries on its northern flank. *Diserth* means a retreat or a deserted place – presumably the hermitage of the local saint Cwyfan, to whom the church is dedicated, along with St Bridget. The church of St Bridget and St Cwyfan may have developed from the original hermit's settlement. It has an elaborate Celtic churchyard cross (now inside the church) and the base of another. The church was virtually rebuilt by the Victorian architect Gilbert Scott in 1873-75, but it still has its magnificent late medieval east window. The upper part of the window depicts the twelve apostles, each carrying an attribute; Peter has his keys, John a palm branch and a chalice (referring to the story in which someone tried to poison him by putting a snake in his wine). Each of the apostles carries a scroll with words from the Apostles' Creed. The lower part of the window is a Tree of Jesse – the earthly family tree of Jesus, with the kings and prophets of Israel in the branches. At the top, the Virgin Mary emerges from a lily into a burst of sunbeams, with the infant Jesus in her arms.

Dyserth Castle. Following the death of Llywelyn ap Iorwerth in 1240, the English extended their authority in northern Wales as far as the Conwy river and began rebuilding castles in the area. About 1245 a new castle was begun by Henry III at Dyserth, in a position of considerable natural strength. It was intended to supplement or replace the first castle at Rhuddlan. Dyserth Castle is also sometimes known as Caerfaelan, Carregfaelan, Castle of the Rock and Castle de Rupe. A castle was perhaps begun very close to the present site in 1238, but the position chosen for the structure must have been unsuitable, for another castle was built in 1241. The castle was attacked by the Welsh in 1245, and later destroyed by Llywelyn ap Gruffudd in 1263. Most of the castle has been quarried away but the remains of the redoubt can be seen as a small rectangular clearing amongst the trees just to the left of the cliff face. The dry moat can also be seen.

Eagle and Child Inn. Built as a farmhouse in the early part of the 19th century, it has been an inn for more than 100 years. It takes its name from the crest of the Stanley family, sometime Lords of the Manor.

Gwaenysgor. The name comes from *gwaun*, Welsh for uplands, and the Danish word *scor* for steep hill, suggesting it was a 10th century Scandinavian outpost. Nearby is Home Farm estate with its Elizabethan mansion, occupied for many years by the Morgan family who supported Charles I during the Civil War. Gop Hill, near the village is the second largest tumuli, or burial mound, in Britain, raised probably as a memorial to people buried in the caves below. Exploration of these caves in 1886 uncovered a sealed chamber containing Neolithic and Bronze Age human skeletons. Woolly rhinoceros, wolf and other prehistoric remains have also been found here.

Offa's Dyke. Offa was King of Mercia from 757 to 796 AD. His kingdom covered the area between the Trent/Mersey rivers in the north to the Thames Valley in the south, and from the Welsh border in the west to the Fens in the east.

Offa's Dyke is a linear earthwork which roughly follows the Welsh/English boundary. It consists of a ditch and rampart with the ditch on the Welsh-facing side, and appears to have been carefully aligned to present an open view into Wales from along its length. Originally it was about thirty yards (27m) wide and nine yards (8m) from the ditch bottom to the bank top. The dyke appears to have been constructed in response to events in the border region, but whether it was intended as an agreed boundary, as a defensive structure with long lost additional fortifications or for some other use is not known. It is thought to have been started in about 785 AD and to have taken several years to build. Much of the dyke is still traceable along the eighty miles. In places it still retains most of its original dimensions while in other parts it has disappeared due to 1200 years of farming activity and its presence can only be detected by archaeological work.

Prestatyn. An important feature of the town is the Roman bath house, with three rooms, two being heated from a furnace at the western end of the building. Next to the bath house, excavation revealed three Roman timber buildings, dating to the second century, being perhaps bronzesmith's workshops as 16 bronze brooches were found there. Lead working and glass or enamel working also took place there. A Roman port possibly existed on the western edge of the town.

Prestatyn castle was built by Henry II in 1157. Owain Gwynedd razed both the castle and the surrounding town to the ground in around 1167. Today, all that remains of the castle is a low mound and stone pillar. At that time, Prestatyn was a small commote, consisting of a number of cottages around the castle, belonging to the Earl of Chester. It had its own market place, mill, blacksmith's shop and a granary.

Before the opening of the Chester to Holyhead railway in the mid 19th century, the economy of the Prestatyn area was agriculture, the extracting of silver, lead and zinc and the quarrying of limestone. The railway opened the area up to tourism, and with other improvements in communication, the town developed as a home for commuters working in the coal, steel and textile industries of Flintshire.

Pant y Fachwen cottage. It was built about 200 years ago. It had two rooms, with a fireplace in one, which was probably the kitchen. In the outhouse, there would probably have been a boiler to wash clothes and an oven to bake bread. There was about an acre and a half of land with the cottage. Many mining families lived here over the years until the estate was closed towards the end of the 1870s. In 1791, a 58 year old lead miner living here was killed when he fell down a shaft in nearby Talargoch mine. In the 1871 census, the cottage was home to a miner, his wife and nine children, aged between five months and 19 years old. Bushes and trees grew over the remains of the cottage until the 1990s when work on Offa's Dyke Path exposed the ruins. The foundations were dug and then secured.

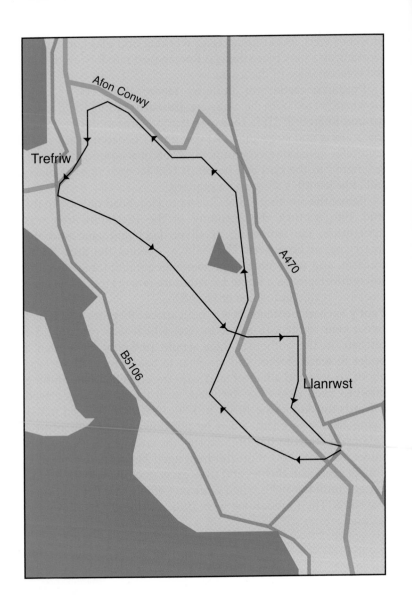

8. Tu Hwnt i'r Bont, Llanrwst

Tu Hwnt i'r Bont

This National Trust owned property, shrouded by virginia creeper, is a former courthouse where Sir John Wynn of nearby Gwydir sat in judgement over the people of Llanrwst. It is now a cafe serving teas, coffees and excellent scones.

The walk – *from the old bridge at Llanrwst to Tu Hwnt i'r Bont and then following the path along afon Conwy to Trefriw and back to Llanrwst.*
4 miles – 1.75 hours (without including a stop at Trefriw)

Start near the old bridge at Llanrwst – **Pont Fawr**; there is space for about half a dozen cars on the Llanrwst side of the bridge. Go over the bridge to Tu Hwnt i'r Bont, and then look for a public footpath sign on the right. Go down the track and after a while you will see a stile on your right. Go over it and follow the path that runs along a ditch in the right hand side of the field. Go over another stile and continue in the same direction past a small lake to another stile. Go over it and straight ahead over a small bridge and over a stile. You will then go over another stile and walk along the **embankment** that runs parallel to **afon Conwy.**

Go over the stile and continue along the embankment towards a bridge. Don't go over the **footbridge** (Pont Gower) nor to the left but go straight ahead over the two stiles and along the embankment. Go through the small gate and continue along the embankment to a stile near some pools. Go over it and continue along the embankment, through two kissing gates and then the path goes to the left away from the river.

Go through the kissing gate and continue along the embankment, then turn left and rejoin the river. Go through two kissing gates and continue along the embankment before turning left towards **Trefriw.** Follow the embankment that now

Trefriw Woollen Mill

70

runs parallel to afon Crafnant, through two kissing gates but don't go over the bridge on your right. Go through the kissing gate to a track and a public footpath sign. Go through the gate and along the path that runs between two fences. Go through two kissing gates and out into the main road at Trefriw. In front of you is the woollen mill. Why not spend some time in Trefriw? There are two pubs here, a cafe, shops and the chalybeate wells.

Turn left and follow the road that goes past a caravan park (not the main road). At the end of the road, follow the path between the playing field and the recreation ground. You will then reach a lane; follow it to the footbridge. Go over this and then straight on towards Llanrwst. When you reach some houses, go right, past the Queens Hotel and then to the main road that runs into Llanrwst. When you reach the car park on your right, you have a choice of two routes. You can go straight ahead to the town square (it is well worth turning right by the Eagles Hotel to visit **St Grwst Church**) and then go back to the bridge where you started the walk, or go into the car park near the Plas y Dre library and look for a Riverside Walk sign. Follow it down the steps and to the left and follow the path alongside the river. You will then go past St Grwst Church and then up the steps near the old bridge and into the centre of town or the car park.

OTHER POINTS OF INTEREST
Afon Conwy. The river rises from Llyn Conwy near Penmachno in Snowdonia and over its 36 mile length drops nearly 1,500 feet before it reaches the coast near Conwy. Its short length makes its level rise and fall very quickly when it rains heavily in the mountains. The river is tidal up to Llanrwst (about 14 miles from the sea) and at one time small ships and boats used to sail as far as here. At the turn of the 20th century pleasure boats came up the river to Trefriw bringing trippers – up to a thousand a day – from Conwy, Llandudno and Deganwy, for fishing, climbing, painting and in the recreation ground golf,

Afon Conwy

tennis, bowls, croquest and quoits. The chalybeate wells have attracted visitors here from the 1800s to take the sulphur-iron rich waters. The wells date back to the Roman period when the Twentieth Legion had its headquarters in Caerhun lower down the valley. During the 19th century the pump room and baths were developed as a curative centre. Trefriw's heyday as a tourist resort ended during the second world war due to silting of the river, but visitors still come here by car and bus to visit the spa baths and woollen mill.

Embankment. The cob was built around 1815 although there have been numerous extensions and improvements since then. The valley was prone to flooding a number of times a year and the ground tended to be waterlogged and difficult to farm. At the beginning of the 19th century, the Reverend Walter Davies described the land as "... a perfect bog, partly peat, partly clay, producing a scanty crop of short and sour hay." The main landowner, the Earl of Ancaster, embarked on a scheme to

Pont Fawr

improve the farmland by digging drainage ditches and enclosing the land with the embankment. Despite the defences, the Conwy broke through the embankment and flooded the area twice in 2004, after very heavy rain.

Pont Gower. The original bridge was a timber trestle construction built in the 19th century to link Trefriw with the railway station in Llanrwst, from where visitors would be taken by horse-drawn carriage to the Trefriw health spa. Some of the timber foundations of the original bridge are still visible underneath the modern suspension bridge.

Pont Fawr. It is believed to have been designed by Inigo Jones and was built in 1636. This graceful triple-arched structure served the ancient counties of Caernarfonshire and Denbighshire as the only valley crossing until the construction of Thomas Telford's iron bridge at Betws-y-coed and suspension bridge at Conwy in the 19th century. Pont Fawr Llanrwst was a vital component in the defence of northern Wales during the

English Civil War and in the latter half of the conflict Royalist troops blew up the western arch of the bridge to halt the advance of Parliamentarian artillery.

Llanrwst – is a town shrouded in myth, legend and a history dating back 1,500 years and having altered very little in the last 400 years. By the tenth century there was a sizeable settlement on this site, which in 954AD saw the brutal and bloody Battle of Llanrwst, a decisive battle between the forces of northern and southern Wales. The town was wasted by an English army in 1403 because of its staunch support of Owain Glyndŵr's revolution and it suffered once again during the Wars of the Roses, when it was completely destroyed by Yorkist troops under the leadership of William Herbert, Earl of Pembroke. The town is proud of its independent roots and found itself in the No Man's Land of past wars. It still bears the motto: 'Cymru, Lloegr a Llanrwst' (Wales, England and Llanrwst). Llanrwst Almshouses were constructed in 1610 by Sir John Wynn of Gwydir to house twelve poor men of the parish. They continued to provide shelter until 1976 when the buildings closed. Then in 1996 with the aid of Heritage Lottery funding they were restored and in 2002 opened as a museum of local history and a community focal point. It consists of two restored period rooms, temporary exhibitions and local artefacts. A working herb garden is situated in the museum grounds.

St Grwst Church. It is dedicated to the Celtic saint Grwst, a sixth century Welsh missionary who settled in Dyffryn Conwy. The present church, although constructed in 1170, dates from 1470, rebuilt two years after its destruction by Yorkist troops. The church houses a beautiful rood screen, a relic of the Cistercian Abbey at Maenan, built in 1509. The Wynn side chapel was built in 1634 as a family mausoleum and houses rare examples of Stuart-period memorials. The chapel is home to the stone sarcophagus of Llywelyn ap Iorwerth, known as Llywelyn Fawr, and the effigy of Hywel Coetmor, a local knight who fought under the Black Prince at Poitiers and returned

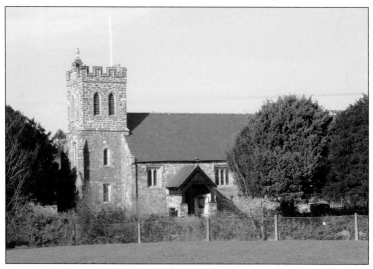

St Grwst Church, Llanrwst

home to participate in the Glyndŵr Rebellion. Both structures are Grade I listed buildings. Open for accompanied viewing are a reproduction of a fresco depicting the Last Supper (from the Santa Maria Monastery in Milan), the ancient Llanrwst Bell and the spur of Dafydd ap Siencyn, the local 15th century outlaw. The church has recently undergone a programme of restoration funded by the Heritage Lottery Fund.

Trefriw. At one time Trefriw was an important trading centre and was regarded as the biggest inland port in Wales. Merchandise was brought up river from the coast and boats returned with slate, ore and timber from the surrounding hills.

It was also an important wool manufacturing centre. The mill was established before the industrial revolution, with its fulling mill taking already woven cloth from the cottages to wash and finish.

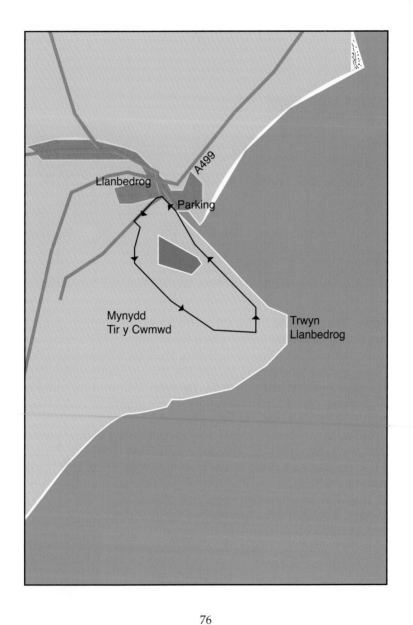

Llanbedrog

A499

Parking

Mynydd
Tir y Cwmwd

Trwyn
Llanbedrog

9. Ϯraeϯh Llaⴖbedrog

The beach at Llanbedrog

The road to Llanbedrog beach, which was bought by the National Trust in 2000, has probably been painted and photographed more often than any area on the peninsula. Ships used to unload coal and lime on the beach here and there are the remains of an old lime kiln on the southern end. The remains on the beach was the slate carrying ship *John and Margaret* which caught fire in 1912 whilst waiting for fair weather to sail. During the English Civil War, Cromwell's army used St Pedrog's Church as a stable. Walls and gravestones were broken as well as an ancient window on the eastern side. The pieces were later kept in a large chest, and when the present church was built in 1865, they were used to form a window on the west side.

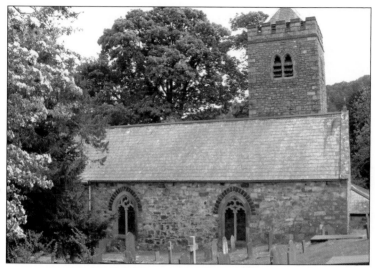
St Pedrog's Church, Llanbedrog

The walk – *from Traeth Llanbedrog, past Plas Glyn y Weddw, to the top of Mynydd Tir Cwmwd and back.*
2.5 miles – 1.5 hours

Park your car in the National Trust car park by the beach. If coming by bus, disembark in the village and follow the signs to Plas Glyn y Weddw and beach, and start your walk from the entrance to the gallery. Otherwise go out of the car park entrance and go to the right, past the entrance to **Oriel Plas Glyn y Weddw**, a shop and St Pedrog's Church – all on the left – and to a junction. Here, go to the left and before reaching the Church Hall, go left again and up the hill and to the right.

Ignore the footpath to the left and continue up the hill and through the trees. You will now come across another footpath on your left, pointing to **Mynydd Tir y Cwmwd**. Follow the track to a junction and go to the right up the slope. Ignore the stile on the left and go straight ahead, through a gate, under an

Daybreak over Pwllheli bay from the top of Mynydd Tir y Cwmwd

arch of trees and to a farmhouse and go straight ahead up the path, through the gate, through the trees and up the steps.

Ignore the path on the left and go straight ahead. Behind you is a magnificent view of the Eifl peaks and Llanbedrog and to the left the Llŷn coast and Pwllheli. Ignore the track on the right and go left. Near a large circular pile of stones go to the right to the trig point on the summit of Mynydd Tir y Cwmwd. In front of you are **Abersoch, Ynysoedd Tudwal** and **St. Tudwal's Roads**. If you followed the path straight ahead of you, you would reach Abersoch.

But after a rest, turn to the left and return to the pile of stones and go right and keep to the right. Continue straight ahead, ignoring the paths to the left and right and down the main path to a post with the sign Llŷn Coastal Path on it. Follow the path down to the left and ignore the narrow path to the right and up to another post and go straight ahead to the **Iron Man sculpture**. Then go to the right to another post with a coastal

Trwyn Llanbedrog

path sign. Go to the right and down the steps until you reach the beach. During an unusually high tide, it may not be possible for you to get onto the beach here, therefore you should ask locally before you start this walk in winter.

Go to the left, past the Boathouse, and then up the steps and to the right. At the junction, go to the right and down past the cottage on the left and to the beach. Go over the stream, to the left and up the hill past the cafe and toilets and back to the car park.

OTHER POINTS OF INTEREST
Abersoch – between 1774 and 1854, 14 ships were built in the harbour here, and coal ships used to unload their cargo on the beach. Abersoch developed as a tourist destination during the second half of the 20th century, due mainly to the excellent sailing in Bae Ceredigion.

Mynydd Tir y Cwmwd. There were three quarries here at one

Oriel Glyn y Weddw

time, producing chippings and setts or paving stones, and a pier, (parts of which remain) was built on the beach to export them. Here also is Ogof Wil Puw, a cave in which a local pirate kept his treasure.

Oriel Glyn y Weddw – was built for Lady Love Jones Parry as a dower house in 1856. She never lived here, but visited it occasionally. In 1896 it was bought by Solomon Andrews, a Cardiff businessman. The house was converted into an art gallery which housed paintings by Gainsborough and Turner and the stableyard was roofed over to form a ballroom which was also used for afternoon teas. Visitors used to arrive by tram from Pwllheli and was one of the main attractions of the area. The property was sold in 1946 and then fell into disrepair until it was bought by Dafydd and Gwyneth ap Tomos who restored the building and opened it again as an art gallery. The house is now owned by a trust.

Iron Man sculpture. The original sculpture was a tin man, a

The Iron Man

figurehead from a ship placed there by Solomon Andrews, owner of nearby Plas Glyn y Weddw. When it was burnt, the village decided to replace it with another one, which was commissioned for £7,000. It was placed in position in 1981, and became known as the Iron Man. However, this was also vandalised so that all that remained were the boots. Again the village decided to replace it, but this time using local village talent. It was placed in position by a helicopter on 1 June 2002. This latest one is hollow and on a windy day the wind makes the Iron Man sing!

St Tudwal's Roads – used to be a safe anchorage for the numerous ships plying their trade along the shores, although a number of sailing vessels did meet an untimely end here. At one time there were plans to build a breakwater from Penrhyn Du to provide extra anchorages and to protect the ships loading ore from the mines but they did not come to fruition.

Ynysoedd Tudwal – are two islands; Ynys Fach is the one nearest the shore and it is said that at one time during a low tide it was possible to walk to it. In 1877 a lighthouse was established here with a white light flashing every twenty seconds and a red light which is seen from the Pwllheli end. The other is Ynys Fawr; it is said that Saint Tudwal lived here at one time and there are the remains of monastic settlements of different periods here. The last monk was Father Henry Bailey Maria

Hughes but he had to leave the island in 1887 when a great storm destroyed his monastery. In the middle if the 20th century, there were plans to establish a nudist colony here but nothing came of them. A few years ago, most of the animals living here died. There used to be Soya sheep here who lived on seaweed, deer and rabbits but the only animals now remaining are black rabbits. Shards of Roman pottery have been found during excavations on both islands. The larger island is owned by television scriptwriter Carla Lane, best known for the comedy series *Liver Birds*.

Abersoch and Cilan from Mynydd Tir y Cwmwd

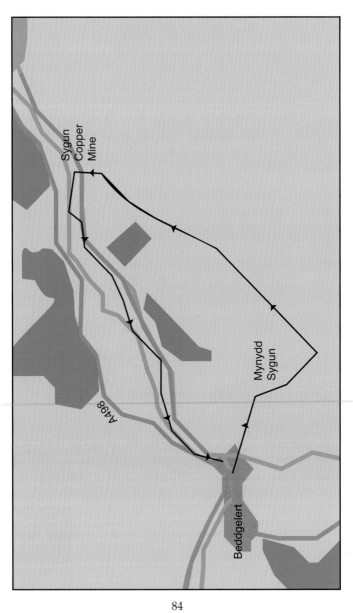

Sygun
Copper
Mine

Mynydd
Sygun

A498

Beddgelert

10. Bwthyn Llywelyn
Tel. 01766 890293

Bwthyn Llywelyn

It is a 17th century cottage, which contains an exhibition and small shop. There is a 1.25 mile circular wheelchair route along the riverbank past Gelert's grave.

The Walk – *from Bwthyn Llywelyn to the top of Mynydd Sygun, down to the Sygun Copper Mine and back to Beddgelert. The first part is quite steep but is well worth the effort especially in May/June and September when you walk through the rhododendron bushes in flower and in August when you walk through the heather.*
6 miles – 3 hours (not including visit to Sygun Copper Mine)

Park your car or come off the bus in the centre of **Beddgelert** and walk towards Bwthyn Llywelyn and the sign to Gelert's Grave. Go past Bwthyn Llywelyn and walk alongside the river,

Bwthyn Llywelyn

past the toilets until you come to a small gate near a bridge. Go through the gate and follow the concrete path alongside the river until you come to a wall, and then go right to a small gate. Go through it and onwards to **Gelert's Grave.**

Retrace your steps back to the start of the concrete path and bridge. On your left is **St Mary's Church.** Go over the bridge and straight ahead between two rows of houses and then left past the house at the end until you come to a public footpath sign. Walk up the hill until you reach Penlan on the left where **Albert Bestall** lived. There is a small gate in front of you. Go through it and up the steep path until you come to a flat ridge.

Follow the footpath to the right until you come to a gate in the wall. Go through it and follow the path to the right and go up to the top of a rock. Here there are wonderful views of Beddgelert below as well as the river Glaslyn and its estuary and Bae Ceredigion in the distance. Then follow the path to the left until you come to the summit of Mynydd Sygun.

Look for a poorly marked path on your left which goes through rocks and then onto marshy ground with a white stone near it. Follow it over the rock and down. Then up and then down to the right until you come to another rock. Don't follow the path to the right but go over the ridge and down the side of the rock. It is a bit dangerous in parts here, therefore you can go down another path towards an old ruin and join the path that comes from the right. Then turn left and follow the path up the slope.

Go over the ridge towards a pile of stones (this is where you would have arrived had you followed the 'dangerous' path). Go right, then past a sign near a ruin until you reach a junction and follow the path down to the left. You will then reach flat ground with a wooden fence and a bench on your left and iron bars on the entrance to an old mine on your right.

Go down the wide path with the wooden fence on the left, through the gate and into the **Sygun Copper Mine** where you can visit the mine or stop for some refreshments.

Leave the copper mine site and turn left down a track which runs alongside a wooden fence (there is a public footpath sign on the fence). Go through the gate and follow the lane past the Crusader Centre sign on your left, past an old milestone on your right and past a house on your left. Proceed until you reach a bridge, but go over the stile near the public footpath sign. Follow the path which runs alongside the river Glaslyn. Go through the small gate and proceed to a kissing-gate and to a crossroads. Go straight ahead, over a bridge and back to Beddgelert.

OTHER POINTS OF INTEREST
Alfred Edmeades Bestall (1892-1986), author and illustrator of Rupert Bear from 1935-1965, was a schoolboy at Rydal Mount in Colwyn Bay from 1904-1911. He stayed with his parents at Trefriw in the Conwy Valley in 1912 and 1913, and during this time visited Beddgelert for the first time. After the First World

The old bridge at Beddgelert

War he stayed almost every year at Penrhiwgoch, Nantgwynant, until he purchased his own cottage, Penlan, in 1956. He lived mainly in Surrey, but stayed at Penlan several times a year. In 1980 Penlan became his permanent home, until cancer prevented him living on his own, and he died peacefully at Wern Nursing Home in 1986, aged 93. He was born to missionary parents in Mandalay, Burma, in 1892. A drawing of the head of a mouse caught in a trap won him a scholarship to the Central School of Arts and Crafts in Birmingham. After demob from the First World War he began illustrating for publications such as *Tatler*, *Eve* and *Punch*. In 1935 he was asked to illustrate and write the Rupert stories for the *Daily Express*. This he did for 30 years and, even after officially retiring in 1965, he contributed to the Rupert Annuals until he was 90.

Beddgelert. The picturesque mountain village started to develop in the late 1700s. Before then there were only trackways criss-crossing the area used by farmers, cattle-drovers and

Prince Llywelyn's Hotel, Beddgelert

copper miners. In the late 1700s a new turnpike road was built from Caernarfon to Dolgellau, through Beddgelert. The present main road from Caernarfon closely follows this route and by 1796 there was also a new Beddgelert bridge. During the Napoleonic wars there was a marked increase in English visitors and artists to northern Wales and in 1803 the new Beddgelert (now Royal Goat) Hotel was built to accommodate them. The hotel manager, with local men, created Gelert's grave, and it has attracted visitors ever since. In 1805 another new turnpike road was built, going from Nefyn through Beddgelert and the Nantgwynant valley to join the main road at Capel Curig.

Beddgelert was soon frequented by climbers, walkers and artists and by the 1840s most of the terraced cottages and guesthouses along the Caernarfon and Capel Curig roads had been built. The part of the village between the Royal Goat Hotel and the church was mainly built in the 1900s, although Bwthyn Llewelyn may date to the late 1500s and Church Street to the

Gelert's Grave

early 1800s.

It was the 1860s before the terraces and guesthouses across the river Glaslyn were erected, and in the 1950s a new bridge gave vehicular access. A short-lived narrow gauge railway was built in the 1920s from Dinas near Caernarfon to Porthmadog through Beddgelert to transport slate and copper, but by the time it opened most of the mines and quarries in the area were closing. The line was bought by rail enthusiasts in the 1990s and opened from Caernarfon to Dinas in 1997, hoping eventually to reach Porthmadog.

Gelert's Grave. Llywelyn I (Llywelyn Fawr – the Great) would come to Nantgwynant in summer to hunt. With his dogs he and his men would chase wild boar, deer and wolves up in the mountains. His favourite dog was Gelert, who not only would fight the fiercest of beasts but was also kind to children.

One day Llywelyn and his wife and followers had gone to hunt leaving their child in the care of the maid. But once she

90

heared the sound of the horn up in the mountains, she left the baby in its cradle and went out for a walk. Llywelyn suddenly realised that Gelert was not with him. He was sure that something had happened to it and he decided to return home.

As they reached the palace, Gelert came out with his tail wagging, but there was blood on its face. Llywelyn rushed into the palace and found the cradle overturned with the bedclothes on the floor and no sign of the baby. He was

St Mary's Church

certain that Gelert had killed him. Llywelyn pulled out his sword and plunged it into his faithful dog, killing it instantly.

Then Llywelyn heard a baby cry. One of his men picked up the cradle and there they saw the baby, unharmed. They picked up some of the bedclothes, and found a huge wolf, dead.

Llywelyn realised what he had done. Gelert had killed the wolf and saved his son. He carried Gelert's body to a nearby field and buried him before placing a mound of stones on his grave.

But there is no truth in this story. Beddgelert is named after Saint Celer. There is no grave there and the story was invented in the 19th century by the owner of the Royal Goat Hotel in order to attract more visitors to the village.

St Mary's Church. The first people to settle in the area were Christian missionaries who probably arrived by sea around 700 AD and established a hermitage on the west bank of the Afon

Sygun Copper Mine

Colwyn. Their leader may have been Celer, whose grave later gave the village its name. This early Christian community was by 1200 famous for its holiness and hospitality to travellers. By 1230 the community was re-formed as the Augustinian Priory of the Valley of St Mary of Snowdon and the Welsh princes gave them lands and paid for the new stone priory church, parts of which can still be seen. Around 1200 the land north of the rivers Glaslyn and Colwyn had been given by Llywelyn Fawr to the Cistercians of Aberconwy. After Henry VIII closed all the monasteries in the 1530s, the priory church was made the parish church of the new parish of Beddgelert. The crown owned the land but by 1600 had sold it to local Welshmen who divided it into various estates.

The present church consists of a nave and chancel from the 13th century, with a 19th century north transept and vestry on the site of an earlier aisle. The earliest masonry, of which the principal remains are the three light east window and the two bay arcade, date from around 1230.

Sygun Copper Mine. In this 19th century mine, which is open to the public, there are winding tunnels and large, colourful chambers, magnificent stalactite and stalagmite formations and copper ore veins which contain traces of gold, silver and other precious metals. The beautiful countryside captured the imagination of movie makers, who turned the mountainside surrounding Sygun into a Chinese village in 1958 for the filming of *The Inn of the Sixth Happiness*, starring the late Ingrid Bergman.

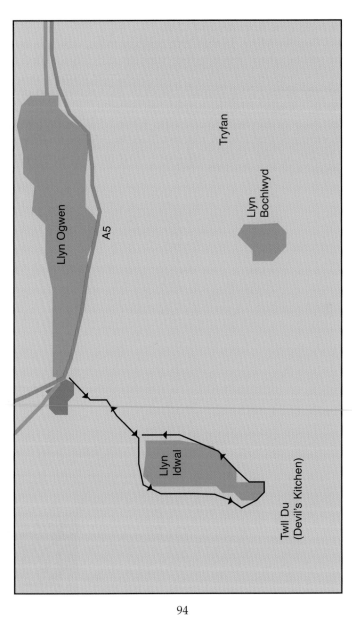

11. Cwm Idwal

Winter ice on the waters of Cwm Idwal

Cwm Idwal is a nature reserve. The landforms attract geologists as it is the best place to see the effects of crushing and folding that took place around 450 million years ago when the northern and southern halves of Britain crashed together and pushed up these mountains.

The effects of the Ice Age are also seen here. The cwm was carved by a huge glacier which sat on the slope and by a tongue of ice which flowed from the summit over the rocky cliffs of Twll Du or Devil's Kitchen. On some of the rocks, the pattern of ice scratches show the direction in which the glaciers moved off the mountain.

Botanists visit the cwm to study the rare arctic-alpine plants, such as moss campion, mountain avens, Welsh poppy, alpine lady's mantle, Snowdon Lily and purple saxifrage, that grow in crevices in the rocks. Charles Darwin once visited here.

During the 1960s and 1970s the Countryside Commission for Wales experimented with excluding grazing from small fenced areas. By now, heather flourishes here as well as flowering plants and grasses. In 1998 sheep were removed from the nature reserve to protect the plants. A shepherd is employed to try and keep sheep from the cwm.

Birds such as chough, ring ouzel, wheatear, raven and peregrine falcon are seen here, and in the streams running into Llyn Idwal are dipper and grey wagtail.

Many visitors come to walk around the lake and to climb on the famous Idwal Slabs.

The walk – *from Bwthyn Ogwen, around Llyn Idwal, and back*
3 miles – 2 hours

Go up the A5 from Bethesda towards Capel Curig until you come to Llyn Ogwen on your left and **Pont Ogwen** and **Bwthyn Ogwen** and a car park on your right. To the left of the cafe is a path, follow it up to a stile. Go over it and then over the footbridge to a fork. Go right and walk along the path to Llyn Idwal.

Near the lake is a footbridge, cross it and through the gate and then left and follow the edge of the lake. When you reach a small beach, walk along it rather than following the path to the right. You will then reach a wall and a gate. Go through the gate and follow the rocky path straight ahead. You can turn left here and follow the edge of the lake; there are bits of path here but it can be a bit wet.

Otherwise follow the path up to the Devil's Kitchen, the large, dark rocks in front of you. When you have almost reached them, look for a path to your left which takes you down to the edge of the lake where you will meet the path that goes along the shore. To your right are the Idwal Slabs, with most probably climbers on them.

Follow the path until you reach the footbridge where you

turned right on the way up, and go straight down to the car park.

The legend of Llyn Idwal. During the 12th century, Owain ap Cynan was Prince of Gwynedd. He had 19 sons, but his favourite was Idwal, a handsome boy. When Idwal was still young, fighting broke out between his father and Hywel, King of Powys, and there was the possibility that the men of Powys would attack Gwynedd. Owain wanted a refuge for Idwal; he was also keen for him to learn how to write poetry and to play the harp. Owain knew of a man called Nefydd, a poet and harpist who lived in a large house near Capel Curig. Idwal would be safe there and he would learn Nefydd's crafts.

Nefydd was known as Nefydd Hardd (the Handsome), and he was determined that his son Dunawd would grow up to be handsome and gifted like himself. But this was not to be. Idwal and Dunawd would play together and the people of the area had noticed that Idwal was much more gifted and handsome than his playmate. Nefydd had also noticed this and he started thinking about how he could get rid of Idwal, but he was afraid of harming him lest Owain would hear of it.

Dunawd was very jealous of Idwal and it didn't take much persuading by his father for him to take Idwal up into the mountains and throw him into one of the lakes. The two boys went along Dyffryn Ogwen and up the slope to the circular lake surrounded by steep rocks. They walked around the lake and when they had reached the far end, underneath the dark rocks, Dunawd pushed Idwal into the lake where he soon drowned in the dark, icy water.

Gate on Cwm Idwal's footpath

Nefydd sent a message to

The path to Cwm Idwal, above Bwthyn Ogwen

Owain to tell him of the tragedy. When he heard the news it filled him with grief, but he was suspicious of Nefydd's story. He sent his men to interrogate Nefydd but they learnt nothing. Nevertheless, Owain decided to punish Nefydd and took his grand house from him.

Ever since the drowning of Idwal in the lake above Dyffryn Ogwen, it has has been known as Llyn Idwal and it is said that no bird will fly over its dark waters after the tragic drowning of the prince's son.

OTHER POINTS OF INTEREST
Pont Ogwen. This bridge was built by Thomas Telford during the construction of the A5 from London to Holyhead and is about 200 years old. Underneath it is another bridge, going back to Roman times.

Bwthyn Ogwen. Early in 1964 Bwthyn Ogwen was bought by Birmingham Education Authority. During the summer of 1964 one of its instructors fell off a new route on Clogwyn Du. During his rescue by a hastily formed party, it was soon realised that there was a need for a dedicated mountain rescue team. The Ogwen Valley Mountain Rescue Team was conceived in the autumn of that year, made up of the Bwthyn Ogwen staff, Mountaineering Club of North Wales, Bangor University Mountaineering Club and a few other regulars.

During 1966 the team was based in a caravan behind Bwthyn Ogwen, and in 1976, the team moved into a small front room with a lean-to shed for the equipment store. The rescue team took it over completely in 1988 after renovating it. The building was set out so that it could be shared with the National Trust volunteers who stay for working holidays.

The rescue team have between 50 and 70 callouts per year. There are approximately 50 people on the team, all volunteers. Many team members are qualified to a high standard of First Aid. Although they are completely independent of the police, they usually work with them at their request. Their usual response time to an incident is typically 20 minutes before deploying someone on to the hill and a full team callout can be effected within 30 minutes.

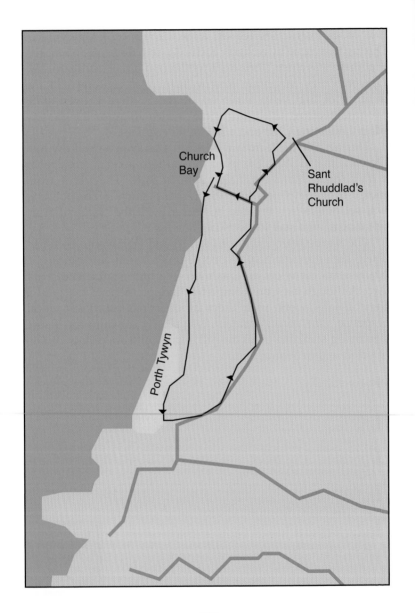

Church
Bay

Sant
Rhuddlad's
Church

Porth Tywyn

12. Bwthyn Swtan

Bwthyn Swtan

Bwthyn Swtan was the last thatched cottage on Ynys Môn, and was occupied until 1975. It is owned by the National Trust but has been leased to Cyfeillion Swtan (*Friends of Swtan*), a local conservation group, who received European funds to rebuild it stone by stone in 1998/9 using traditional methods and materials. Rough cut trunks and branches (or driftwood from shipwrecks in times gone by) make ridge, cruck rafters and purlins with a base layer of gorse or heather lying on hazel laths. Cyfeillion Swtan has won an award for its contribution to the local environment and heritage.

It is believed that the cottage is about 400 years old. According to records, a family of six lived here at one time as well as a lodger.

The walk – *from Porth Swtan along the shore to Porth Tywyn and then back along a narrow country road with a choice of going straight back to the car park or visiting a headland for magnificent views of the coastline before returning.*
1 or 1.5 hours – 3 or 5 miles

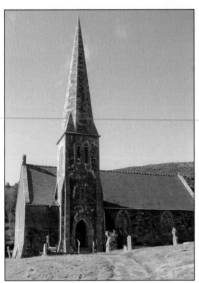
St Rhuddlad's Church

Park your car in the **Porth Swtan** (Church Bay) car park near the toilets. You might like to visit Bwthyn Swtan before you start your journey. Leave the car park and walk downhill until you come to the cafe. Turn left, go through two kissing-gates, and along the coastal path to Porth Penrhyn with its white cottage. Proceed along the coastal path. You will come to some concrete steps and footbridge. Don't go over the stile on your left, but when the tide is out you

Traeth Swtan

can go down the gully on your right to the beach and walk along it.

Otherwise, walk along the coastal path. After passing a cluster of houses on your left, go down the path on your right to the beach at Porth Tywyn. Just after the house on the edge of the beach at the far end you will see a path going inland to a road, follow it. Turn left at the junction and go along the road. You will eventually see an old **windmill** to your right.

Go downhill to a junction. Now you can either go down to Porth Swtan car park which is a few minutes away or carry on along the road and up the hill where there are magnificent views. If you choose the second option, go along the road, downhill, then uphill past the Church Bay Inn on your right and then **St Rhuddlad's Church** on your left.

Just before the church, you will see a footpath sign. Go up the track to the top of the hill. You will then see a footpath to your left over a stile. Here there are wonderful views of Porth Swtan,

Two of Anglesey's old mills

the coast and Mynydd Twr (Holyhead Mountain) ahead of you. Follow the footpath down the fields towards the sea until you reach the coastal path which takes you back to Porth Swtan car park.

OTHER POINTS OF INTEREST

Porth Swtan (*Church Bay*). Swtan is Welsh for whiting (a fish) but since the spire of St Rhuddlad's Church was so prominent from the sea, a marine chart of 1816 called it Church Bay.

St Rhuddlad's Church. Rhuddlad was the daughter of the King of Leinster in Ireland, whose feast is on the 4th of September. The present church was built in 1858 and unusually for Ynys Môn it has a spire.

Windmill. In 1861 there were over a hundred windmills on Anglesey, but most fell into disuse between 1856 and 1900 when they could not compete with the steam driven mills introduced in the cities by the industrial revolution. When mill machinery

Bwthyn Swtan

broke down it was not repaired or replaced and by now ruined mill towers without caps are a feature of Anglesey. One mill, Melin Llynnon, was bought by the county council and repaired a few years ago. It is possible to visit it and buy freshly milled Melin Llynnon flour.

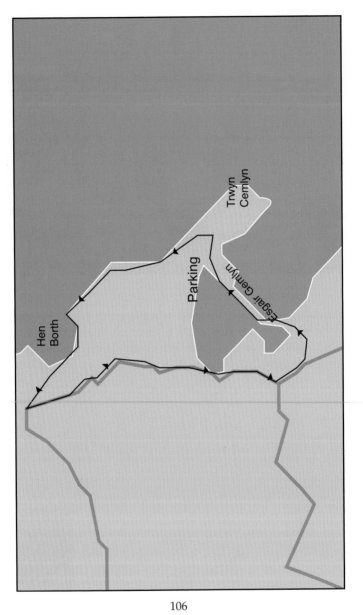

Trwyn Cemlyn

Parking

Esgair Gemlyn

Hen Borth

13. Cemlyn

Cemlyn lagoon

Centuries of storms depositing pebbles high up on the beach created the shingle ridge, and the weir built in the 1930s at the western end has formed a lagoon which is fed by freshwater streams and the incoming tide. A large colony of sandwich terns breed in the lagoon, along with common, arctic and roseate terns. Red-breasted merganser, shelduck, mallard, coot, moorhen, oystercatcher, redshank, reed bunting and sedge warbler can be seen on the reserve. Large numbers of wildfowl such as goldeneye and little grebe winter here. On the shingle ridge there is sea campion, thrift, yellow horned poppy and sea kale. The reserve was in private ownership until it was bought by the National Trust in 1971 and leased to the North Wales Wildlife Trust.

Lighthouse on Ynysoedd y Moelrhoniaid

The walk – *from Cemlyn Nature Reserve along the beach towards Ynysoedd y Moelrhoniaid (Skerries) and back to Cemlyn beach via paths and narrow lanes.*
3 miles – 1 hour

Go to the car park on the left hand side (western side) of Cemlyn Nature Reserve near **Bryn Aber**. Walk along the track towards the beach, go through a gap near a gate and you will reach the monument that commemorates the 150th anniversary of the launching of the first **lifeboat** in northern Wales. **Wylfa Power Station** is to your right. Follow the path on the shore to the left.

Go over a stile and walk along the edge of the field uphill to a kissing-gate. Again go along the edge of the field to another kissing-gate. You will now see **Ynysoedd y Moelrhoniaid** (*The Skerries*) and the flashing lighthouse out at sea to your right.

Go downhill to another kissing gate and on to where there is a gate going to the beach. Turn left and go inland along a path that runs along the side of a fence towards a farmhouse. Go through the gate and left onto a lane. Walk past the lagoons on your left to a junction and then turn right. At the next junction, near the National Trust sign, go left and uphill past a farmhouse.

Walk downhill to a 'Give Way' sign. Go left here. At the junction near the white house on your left, go straight ahead until you come to a small car park near the beach. Turn left here and either walk along the pebbly beach or walk along the footpath that runs alongside the lake. During the nesting season you will have to walk along the beach.

When you reach a building you will have to cross a stream over a concrete embankment. Either go left along the rocks skirting the wall (which may be difficult at high tide) or go around the building to your right and then back into the car park where you started from.

OTHER POINTS OF INTEREST

Bryn Aber. It is the former home of millionaire Captain Vivian Hewitt. He was a passionate bird watcher and egg collector, and he built the weir at Cemlyn to form a lagoon. The high walls around the house were built to protect the trees and garden

Stone commemorating the 150th anniversary of the launching of the first lifeboat in northern Wales

from the salt-laden winds and to provide a bird sanctuary. Hewitt was also a pioneer aviator and made the first flight from Britain to Ireland in 1912. During the Second World War there were rumours that he was supplying German U-boats with fuel and he was investigated, but the tanks on his land only contained water. He died in 1965 and his land was later bought by the National Trust.

Lifeboat commemoration. Frances Williams, the local rector's wife, watched helplessly as a ship drifted into Maen y Bugail (West Mouse) only a mile offshore. Forty people drowned in the incident. She immediately started a fund to provide a lifeboat which was launched at Cemlyn in 1828, the first in northern Wales. Her husband, the Rev James Williams became the cox. He was later awarded a gold medal by the RNLI for saving the lives of five people in Cemaes Bay, not in a lifeboat, but by riding his horse into the sea to throw a rope to them.

Wylfa Nuclear Power Station. Construction began in 1963 and reactor number one started generating electricity in January 1971 with reactor number two starting six months later. During construction up to 3,000 men were employed here. It has a permanent staff of around 600 producing 23mKWH of electricity – enough to meet the needs of two cities the size of Liverpool. It is due to close in 2010.

Ynysoedd y Moelrhoniaid (The Skerries). The Welsh name means the islands of the seals, and they were given the name The Skerries by the Vikings. The rock on which the lighthouse stands is at the end of a strip of submerged land which is directly in the path of the major shipping lanes to Liverpool. The first lighthouse was coalfired and established in 1714. Originally a private venture, it was bought by Trinity House in 1841. It was converted to electricity in 1927 and to automatic operation in 1987.

In 1881 the sailing vessel *Gilbert Thompson* was under tow on the last part of her journey between Calcutta and Liverpool but as the ships were negotiating the channel between Ynysoedd y

Moelrhoniaid and Maen y Bugail, the *Gilbert Thompson* keeled over in the strong tide and her iron hull was torn on jagged underwater rocks. All the crew of 22, except a cabin boy with a broken leg, managed to scramble to safety on the rocks before the vessel sank. The men were rescued by the tug and taken to Liverpool.

The most important vessel to perish on these rocks was the royal yacht *Mary*, which belonged to Charles, Pretender to the English throne. She was employed to carry important passengers between Ireland and England. In March 1675 she capsized near the rocks but her long mainmast touched the shore and 39 passengers and crew were able to reach safety, but 36 – including the Earl of Meath – lost their lives. The *Mary's* bronze guns were found by divers in 1971 and are now in the Maritime Museum in Liverpool along with coins, jewellery, tableware and even a woman's skeleton.

The bonesetters of Anglesey. According to legend a smuggler came across two small boys adrift in a boat near the Skerries on a stormy night. One child died but the other was taken ashore and to a house called Mynachdy (if you proceed westwards along the coastal path instead of turning inland you will reach Mynachdy about half a mile inland from Hen Borth), the home of Dr Lloyd. The boy was given the name Evan; it was believed that he was Spanish as he spoke no Welsh or English. As he grew up (he had by now been given the surname Thomas) it was noticed, after he mended the broken leg of a chicken, that he had great skill in setting bones and his reputation spread all over Ynys Môn. Within a few generations there were 21 members of his family who were either doctors or bonesetters.

His grandson – another Evan – set up in practice in Liverpool and his son Hugh Owen Thomas, again a doctor, devised surgical instruments and what became known as the Thomas splint. His surgery became known as the birthplace of modern orthopaedic surgery.

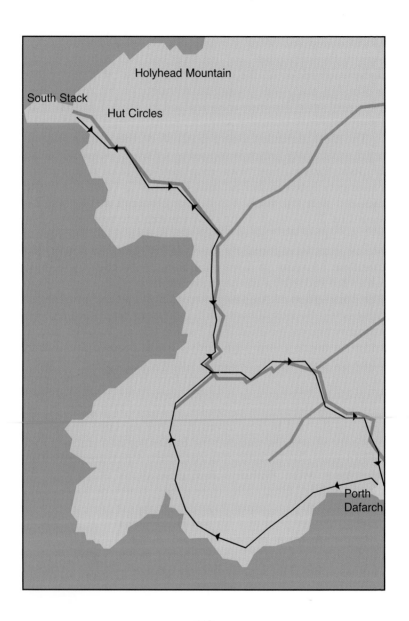

South Stack

Holyhead Mountain

Hut Circles

Porth
Dafarch

14. Porth Dafarch

Porth Dafarch

It is a small sandy cove surrounded by a rocky headland, with rock pools and a coastal footpath. Picnic tables are provided at the beach. Some say that the name Dafarch comes from *dau farch* (two steeds), but this is disputed by academics who say that it possibly refers to the personal name Tafarch, although this is not a common name.

Between 1819 and 1820 this is where the ferries to Ireland left from. It was also used when adverse winds in Holyhead harbour made that inaccessible.

The walk – *from Porth Dafarch westwards along the clifftop path towards South Stack Lighthouse and Mynydd Twr (Holyhead Mountain) and then back along a narrow, winding road, or you can visit the lighthouse and hut circles near Mynydd Twr.*
3.5 miles – 1.5 hours or if you go to the South Stack Cafe 6.5 miles – 3 hours

Go to Porth Dafarch and park here – there are plenty of parking spaces here, although it will be packed on a sunny day in summer. A bus service also passes here, and although there is no bus stop you can ask the driver to set you down. Go down to the beach and go right (as you look out to sea). On the wall is a plaque – and another further along – to **Morswyn** who composed the well known hymn 'Rock of Ages'. You will now see the Coastal Path sign, follow it to the left and go along the path above the beach. Go over the stone stile and you will see a number of paths ahead of you – you can choose any one. Why not follow the one nearest the sea?

The path then goes towards Graig Lwyd headland and then down towards a wooden bridge and then left over a wooden stile. Follow the path up the field to a kissing gate. Go through it and follow the path to the left.

The path now forks – you can choose either one and go up the rock or otherwise. To your left is an ancient fort. Follow the path up the gentle slope to a kissing gate. Go through it and follow the path to the left along the cliff top. Ignore the path to the right.

You now come to a junction, go to the right and aim for a house. You will then come to a car park. Go across it and along the lane and you will come to a narrow road.

You now have a choice. Either turn right and go back along the road to Porth Dafarch or go left towards South Stack and **Mynydd Tŵr** which will take an extra hour and a half. If you intend to return to Porth Dafarch, turn right and follow the instructions from * onwards.

Graig Lwyd

114

Otherwise, turn left and go along the narrow road until you come to a Coastal Path sign on your right. The path runs parallel to the road. Follow it by going over the stone stile and through two gates to the far end when it turn left and goes down towards a stone stile. Go over it and then straight ahead up the hill.

Continue up the hill and at the top you will see on your right a sign marked 'Hut Circles' leading to **Tŷ Mawr Hut Circles**; why not visit them? (I have not included a visit to the hut circles in the total time and miles, but it should not take more than half an hour at the most to visit the huts.) On your left is a car park, go across it and along one of the paths to **Ellin's Tower**, a bird watching centre. In front of you is **South Stack Lighthouse**. Go up the slope to the South Stack Cafe – you can buy a ticket here to visit the lighthouse (I haven't included the time to visit the lighthouse – but it will take at least an hour to go there and back and have a good look around – remember that there are more than 400 steps to go down – and then back up!).

After a cuppa or a picnic, go back down the hill and at the junction go straight ahead over the stone stile and follow the path that runs parallel to the road. Go through the two gates and over the stone stile and out into the road and you will reach the point where you entered the road after walking along the path along the coast *.

Follow the road, past an old chapel on your left. Ignore the turning to the right and continue until you come back to Porth Dafarch.

OTHER POINTS OF INTEREST
Caer y Twr. On the summit of Mynydd Twr is a prehistoric hill fort with an area of about three acres (seven hectares). The fort's good natural position meant it scarcely needed any additional defences but it nevertheless has a large stone defensive wall on the north and east sides – which has survived to a height of three yards (metres) in places. The site is also well defended by

the rocky terrain surrounding the entrance, which is at the north-east corner. The fort's defences have been broken down, perhaps by the Romans who subsequently used the site for a Roman watchtower intended to provide advance warning of Irish sea raiders. From here signals would have been sent by semaphore via a series of signal towers to the Roman legionary fortress at Chester. The base of the watchtower is still visible today.

Ellin's Tower. *Ellin's Tower* was built in 1868 by W O Stanley MP of Penrhos. After falling into disrepair between the two world wars, the tower was bought and restored by the Royal Society for the Protection of Birds in the 1980s. It now gives information on wildlife and local history and provides spectacular views via a closed circuit camera attached to the cliffside. In summer over 4,000 pairs of seabirds nest at South Stack cliffs. From Ellin's Tower you can watch puffins, fulmars, guillemots and razorbills, using binoculars and telescopes, and see live pictures

Remains of one of the huts at Tŷ Mawr.

Ellin's Tower

of the birds on the cliffs.

Morswyn. Samuel Jonathan Griffith (Morswyn) wrote the hymn 'Rock of Ages' inspired by the scenery at Porthdafarch. Morswyn lived in Kingsland, Holyhead. He and his wife Jane suffered the loss of both their children Ifan Huw (1877-1880) and Jane Elin (1882). Morswyn also died at a young age in August 1893 and was buried at Maes Hyfryd cemetery, Holyhead. Morswyn School in Holyhead was named after him.

Mynydd Twr (Holyhead Mountain). Some of the oldest rocks in Britain are found in Anglesey, and on Mynydd Twr Precambrian strata forms the island's highest point. Due to its elevated position, the Romans built a watch-tower here. The mountain also housed a semaphore signal station, built in the 1800s, to guide ships on the journey from Holyhead to Liverpool.

South Stack Lighthouse. A navigation aid was first envisaged in 1665 when a petition to erect a lighthouse was presented to Charles II. It was not granted and it was not until 1809 that light appeared on the rock. The lighthouse, erected at a cost of £12,000, was designed by Daniel Alexander and originally fitted with oil lamps and reflectors. Around 1840 a railway was installed so that a lantern could be lowered down the cliff to sea level when fog obscured the main light. In the mid 1870s the lantern and lighting apparatus were replaced by a new lantern, probably a pressurised multiwick oil lamp. In 1909 an early

South Stack lighthouse

Mynydd Twr

form of incandescent light was installed and in 1927 this was replaced by a more modern form of incandescent mantle burner. The station was electrified in 1938. In 1984, the lighthouse was automated and the keepers withdrawn. The light and fog signal are now remotely controlled and monitored from the Trinity House Operational Control Centre in Harwich, Essex.

The chasm between the mainland and the rock was at first traversed by a hempen cable 21 yards (metres) above sea level, along which a sliding basket was drawn carrying a passenger or stores. This system was replaced in 1828 by an iron suspension bridge 1.5 yards (metres) wide and again in 1964 by an aluminium bridge. The present footbridge was completed in mid-1997. The landward approach to the bridge is by descending 400 steps cut into the cliff face. It is now a listed building and open to the public.

SS *Missouri*. This four-masted barque lies in pieces on the sea bed off Porth Dafarch. In February 1886 she was sailing from Boston, USA, to Liverpool with a mixed cargo of live cattle, hides, palm oil and cotton bales. A south-westerly gale blew the ship in dense fog and a snowstorm onto the shore. The crew tried to lighten the load by sending overboard a quarter of the 395 cattle, but they eventually had to abandon ship. Only fifty of the cattle were saved. Some of the cargo was recovered but not before looters had been there and several men were tried and convicted of theft.

Tŷ Mawr Hut Circles. Excavated by WO Stanley in the 1860s, these stone huts are one of Anglesey's best known early settlements. There is evidence of occupation here from as early as the Middle Stone Age (10,000 BC). The buildings seen today have been identified as belonging to the Iron Age. Materials found at the site suggest that this area was occupied as recently as the sixth century, at the time of St Cybi. There were about eight farms here, consisting of round huts and storage places and workshops. It is likely that they ploughed nearby land and milling stones have been found here suggesting that they processed grain. Heaps of seashells have also been found here.

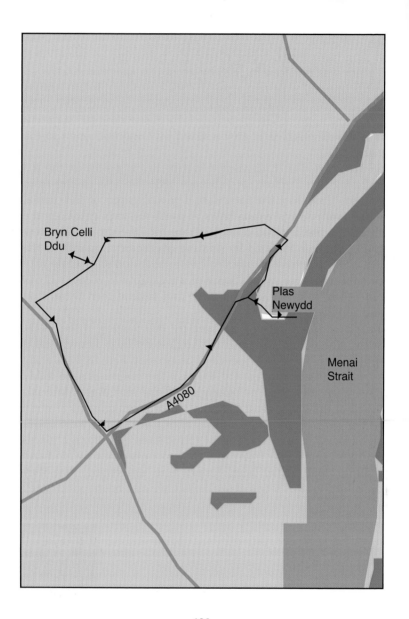

Bryn Celli
Ddu

Plas
Newydd

A4080

Menai
Strait

15. Plas Newydd
Tel. 01248 714795

Plas Newydd

This large mansion, set in about 160 acres, has been the home of the Marquesses of Anglesey and their forebears from the 16th century onwards. The original house was built by the Griffith family, who also built Penrhyn near Bangor. The family were related to the Tudors of Penmynydd, who established the Tudor dynasty on the English throne. The family married into the Bayly and later the Paget families. Parts of Plas Newydd were built with profits from the Parys Copper Mine near Amlwch. The most famous inhabitant was Henry Paget who lost a leg at the Battle of Waterloo and was made the First Marquis of Anglesey due to his skill as a commander of the cavalry and second in command to Wellington. His exploits are chronicled in a military museum in the house. The house also contains a celebrated mural painted between 1936 and 1940 by Rex Whistler, a close friend of the family. There are also a number of family portraits by Whistler, as well as a selection of his work as a book illustrator, stage designer and decorative artist. There is a fine spring garden in the grounds and Australasian arboretum with shrubs and wild flowers as well as a summer terrace and later hydrangeas and autumn colour.

The walk – *from Plas Newydd to Bryn Celli Ddu Burial Chamber and back by an other route.*
5 miles – 2.25 hours

Park your car in the Plas Newydd car park (a bus service passes the main entrance and there is a bus stop nearby.) Go back to the main road, turn right and walk carefully, single file facing the traffic – some cars travel quite fast on this road. Go past a house on the right and the past a sign for the Sea Zoo, Parc y Foel Farm and Plas Newydd.

Go round the bend and then look for a footpath sign on the left. Follow it over a cattle grid and up the lane. Go over another cattle grid, past Llwyn Onn farm on the right to a well-constructed wall. Go left over the style and walk with the wall towards the right hand side of a pine forest to a style and gate. Go over the style and across the field towards Bryn Celli Ddu farm. Go past a ruin on your left to a fence with a gate and style. Go over the style and towards the farm.

You will now reach a footbridge; don't go over it but go left following the fence and the stream towards two styles and a footbridge. Go over them and then right over another footbridge and follow the path to **Bryn Celli Ddu Burial Chamber.**

Go back along the path, over the footbridge and then right and follow the path until you reach the main road. Go left here.

Walk along the road, past a house on the left and up a hill. Go past three other houses and before reaching another two you will see a public footpath sign on your right. Follow it up a lane, through a gate and past a house on the right to Glanyrafon farm. Go to the right before reaching the farmhouse. Go through the gates and then left and through another gate and along a track to another gate. Go through it and along the edge of the field to a stream. Look for a small stile on your right. Go over it, through thorn bushes and then through a gate on your left to another field. Go over the stile and then along the right hand side edge of the field towards Cwr Du house.

Go over a stile and through a gate and to a track near the house. Go left along the track up the hill. Go through a gate, a farmyard and another gate and out to the main road. Go left and once again walk single file facing the traffic.

Go past a house on the right and Llanedwen sign on the left and then the sign to **Moel y Don** on the right and back to the Plas Newydd car park.

OTHER POINTS OF INTEREST
Bryn Celli Ddu Burial Chamber ('the mound in a dark grove'). It is the best passage grave in Wales. It started as a late Neolithic henge or ritual enclosure, with a stone circle surrounded by a bank and internal ditch. A later passage grave was built inside the ditch; the north-east entrance to the burial chamber is retained by a kerb of stones, which, along with the dry-stone walling of the outer passage, creates an elaborate forecourt. The narrow passage is 27 feet (8.2m) long and three feet (0.9m) wide with a low shelf along its north (right) side. This leads to a higher, polygonal burial chamber, eight feet (2.4m) wide, covered by two capstones. In the chamber is a tall, rounded, free-standing pillar, whose purpose is unknown. The spiral carving on the first stone on the left of the chamber entrance may be not authentic.

The whole passage was covered by a cairn, but the existing mound is a partial reconstruction, kept small so that three stones from the old stone circle and two other features behind the

Bryn Celli Ddu

chamber, at the centre of the henge, can be seen. These other features are a pit (in which excavations revealed charcoal and a human ear-bone) and an upright stone carved on both faces and across the top with zigzag and spiral lines. The original pillar is now at the National Museum of Wales in Cardiff, but a replica has been set up in its presumed original position.

The site was visited from 1699, and excavated in 1865 and 1927-31. The passage and chamber excavations revealed both burnt and unburnt human bones, a stone bead, two flint arrowheads, a scraper and mussel shells. Outside the entrance and the ditch, a small, unusual ox burial was found. On the ridge to the north of the site (on the right of the lane as you return) is a tall standing stone.

Moel y Don. Ferries ran from here to the mainland at Y Felinheli from about 400 to 1850 when the Menai Bridge was built. Ships of over one hundred tons were built here towards the end of the 18th century.

Remains of old boat at Moel y Don, with Y Felinheli on the opposite side of the Menai Strait

Some say that the Battle of Moel y Don was fought here in 1282. Edward I's forces had occupied Ynys Môn and prepared to attack the mainland. Amongst his army were Gascon knights and Spanish mercenaries. A bridge of boats was built across the Strait and the army led by the knights started for the mainland. On the opposite shore, the Welsh were well hidden and as the English army started to clamber ashore, they were suddenly attacked. Panic ensued and the English were unable to retreat as men were pouring over the bridge. The boats started swaying and many knights – in full armour – fell into the sea. Others were cut down by Welsh arrows. Then the tide turned, and smashed the bridge of boats. About 30 knights, including their leader Luke de Tany, and over 200 English soldiers perished on that day.

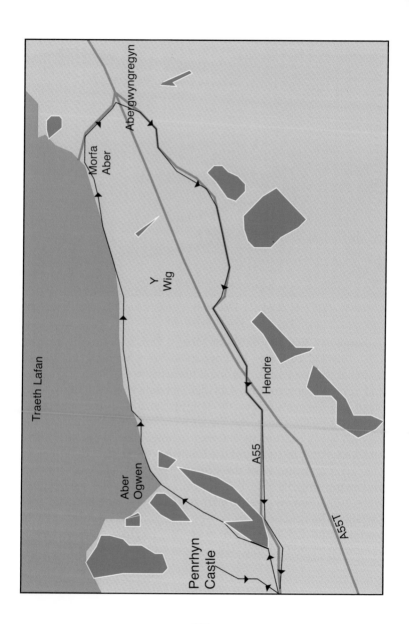

Traeth Lafan

Morfa
Aber

Abergwyngregyn

Y
Wig

Hendre

A55

A55T

Aber
Ogwen

Penrhyn
Castle

16. Penrhyn Castle
Tel. 01248 371337

Penrhyn Castle

The original building was a 15th century square stone fortress with a tower house at one corner. For a time it was the home of the Griffiths family, and one member – Pyrs Gruffudd – was a well known pirate having attacked Spanish ships alongside Sir Francis Drake. The present building is a 19th century fantasy castle built between 1820 and 1845 for the wealthy Pennant family who made their fortune from the slave trade, Jamaican sugar plantations and Welsh slate (they owned the nearby Penrhyn Quarry near Bethesda). The castle contains elaborate carvings and plasterwork and mock-Norman furniture, and an outstanding collection of paintings. There is also a one-ton slate bed made for Queen Victoria. The Victorian kitchen and servants rooms have been restored. There is an industrial museum, model railway museum and

dolls' museum here.

The walk – *from Penrhyn Castle through the picturesque village of Llandygái to Aber Ogwen and along the shore to Abergwyngregyn, returning along the old coast road.*

10 miles – 4.5 hours

Start from the Penrhyn Castle car park and walk to the entrance. (If you don't have a car you can start the walk from the entrance, where there is a bus stop. It will take about twenty minutes to walk from the

Penrhyn Castle

entrance to the castle). Turn left and then left again and into the village of Llandygái. Go through the village towards the school and **St Tegai's Church.** Between these buildings there is a public footpath sign. Follow the path down to a small gate on your right. Go through it and you will come out onto the old A55. Go left over the bridge that crosses **Afon Ogwen.** Ignore the road to the right and go past a private entrance. Ignore another road to the right and go over the railway bridge.

You will then see the Nature Reserve sign pointing left; follow it, over another railway bridge and go past Pentre Isaf, Llwyn Onn and Aber Ogwen farm until you reach the car park on the shore. This is **Aber Ogwen** and the **Spinnies Nature Reserve.** In front of you, on Anglesey, is **Beaumaris** and to the right **Penmon** and **Ynys Seiriol** (Puffin Island).

Turn right and go out of the car park and follow the footpath along the beach. Parts of the path are on stony beach but in some places there is a good path above the beach. Out to sea is **Lafan Sands** which is also a nature reserve. Continue along the shore past a public footpath sign, over an outflow and past the track on the right that leads to **Y Wig.** Continue along the shore, passing an iron stile on the right and you will reach a small bay.

Ahead of you is the large headland of **Penmaenmawr** and to its left the **Great Orme.**

Continue along the shore until you see a track above the shore. Go onto it and follow it past Cwrtiau on the right and you will reach the **Morfa Aber Nature Reserve** car park. This is about half way and an ideal place to have a picnic.

Follow the lane out of the car park, under a railway bridge and when you reach a junction, go to the right. Go up a small hill

Aber Falls

and then follow the sign to **Abergwyngregyn** to the left and then under the A55 Expressway. In front of you is the **Aber Valley**.

You will now reach a crossroads. If you walk about a hundred yards to the left, past the Aber Falls Hotel (a convenient place for a pint or a bite to eat) you will see on your right a house with a large round-topped tower – this is **Pen-y-bryn**. Return to the crossroads and follow the old road in the direction of Bangor past **St Bodfan's Church** on your left. Continue along the road to a crossroads near Y Glyn farm. Go straight ahead past a public footpath sign on your left and down the hill. Go past a farm and down the hill, keeping to the right. Go past a lane to your left and continue down the hill.

At the junction, bear right and at the next junction, bear left and follow the road which runs alongside the A55 Expressway. Go past a lane on your right. To your left is **Hendre Hall,** but bear right and go over the A55 Expressway. Go past a public footpath sign on your right and to a junction. Bear right and walk along the old A55, past an old **turnpike** on your left. Go past two junctions on your left and over a railway bridge, past a junction and a private entrance on the left and over **Afon Ogwen.** Go through the small gate on the right, through Llandýgai and back to the entrance to Penrhyn Castle. Then follow the lane back to the car park.

OTHER POINTS OF INTEREST

Aber Ogwen Nature Reserve. Thousands of waders and wildfowl gather to overwinter here, feeding on shellfish and other invertebrates which live in the shifting muds and sands. Amongst them are shelduck, oystercatcher, curlew and dunlin. During the summer the reeds provide nesting sites for sedge warblers, mallard and moorhen, while flycatchers, bullfinch, chiffchaff, firecrest and blackcap breed in the woodland scrub. From mid-June to mid-September up to 60 swans are to be found here. In autumn and winter, greenshank, redshank, water rail, little grebe, snipe and teal come here to feed and shelter. Kingfishers can be seen here for much of the year feeding in the pools.

Afon Ogwen. The Ogwen flows through the Nant Ffrancon valley in the Snowdonia National Park and is part of the Glyderau Site of Special Scientific Interest. In its upper reaches Afon Ogwen is a high-energy mountain river. The river is the main outflow from Llyn Ogwen, from which it flows northwards over Rhaeadr Ogwen (Ogwen Falls) down into the large U-shaped glacial valley of Nant Ffrancon. Brown trout and sea trout can be found in the river as well as salmon.

Beaumaris. The name comes from Norman-French meaning 'beautiful marsh'. The town and the castle were built by Edward I between 1295 and 1298. A thousand labourers, 400 skilled craftsmen and 200 carters were used to build the castle. In order to build the colonial town, the Welsh villagers of Llan-faes were

Great Orme from Mynydd y Dref, Conwy

moved to Newborough in western Anglesey. The Beaumaris courthouse, opened in 1614, is open to the public as is also the gaol built in 1829.

Great Orme. Four thousand years ago, men using bone, antlers and stone tools mined copper on a large scale here reaching a depth of 300 feet (91m). The mines are now open to the public. There are also prehistoric remains here including Pen y Dinas fort. *The Vikings*, starring Kirk Douglas was partly filmed here and indeed the word Orme, meaning 'sea-monster', comes from their language. One of the features of the Great Orme is the herd of wild goats living there.

Hendre. A Victorian farmyard with cobbled courtyards, established by Lord Penrhyn in around 1860. The Grade 2* buildings have been restored to offer spacious tea rooms with home made food. A number of craft workers are housed in the workshops. The gallery area allows visitors to browse the work of local artisans. In the Victorian tack rooms there are harnesses used by the shire horses when Hendre was a breeding and training farm. Hendre is also considered to be northern Wales' premier dance venue with live bands.

Traeth Lafan. At low tide, people used to walk over the sands to Anglesey before the Menai Suspension Bridge was opened. Guide posts were placed in the sands and there was a rough track of flat stones over the four mile route. Travellers, on foot and horseback, would have to be careful in case they were caught by the tide and many employed the services of a guide. There were only three hours in every twelve when they could

Sailing boats at high tide over Traeth Lafan, between Beaumaris and Aber

cross, and it was impossible in stormy weather. To guide people in mist, the bell in Aber church was tolled for those coming over from Anglesey. On the Anglesey side there is a deep channel (8 metres) and a ferry would be used to cross it. During the 17th century a duel was fought on these sands between Colonel Bulkeley of Baron Hill, Anglesey, and Thomas Cheadle who had worked for him. Bulkeley was killed and Cheadle was hanged at Conwy.

Lafan Sands have been designated a Special Protection Area and Site of Special Scientific Interest. The muds and sands support an abundance of cockles, mussels, lugworms and small fish which in turn attract waders and wildfowls such as oystercatchers, curlew, dunlin and shelduck, especially in winter. The shore provides feeding and safe roosting areas for ducks such as teal and wigeon. Lapwing and redshank also nest here.

The sinking of the *Rothsay Castle*. From 1622 onwards, ships sailed from Liverpool to Beaumaris, becoming eventually a daily service between April and October. The *Rothsay Castle* left Liverpool for northern Wales on 17 August, 1831. But after leaving the port a gale arose and the passengers tried to persuade the captain to turn back but he refused. By midnight they were near Ynys Seiriol (*Puffin Island*) but then it struck Dutchman's Bank, part of the Lafan Sands, and was battered by the wind and waves. It is was also alleged that the ship was unseaworthy and that the captain was drunk. About 130 people lost their lives that night with only 23 surviving.

Morfa Aber Nature Reserve. During autumn, winter and spring, numerous wading birds such as oystercatchers, curlew, lapwing, shelduck, wigeon, mallard and teal feed on the mudflats and saltmarsh. In summer there are a variety of ducks on the pools and swallows and housemartins skim the surface of these pools catching insects.

Penmon. Llywelyn Fawr bequeathed land to build a monastery here. Although many of the buildings are ruins, the church still holds services here. Near the church is a dovecote from the 1600s.

Opposite Ynys Seiriol are old coastguard cottages and a lifeboat station. The first lifeboat came here in 1831 but it was moved to Moelfre in 1848. The present lifeboat station was built in 1880 but the lifeboat was moved to Beaumaris in 1914. The lighthouse on Trwyn Du was built after the sinking of the *Rothsay Castle*. It had two keepers, but since 1922 it has been automatic. It has used solar panels since 1996.

Penmaen-mawr. There has been a quarry here since Neolithic times. Axe-heads and other implements from its distinctive stone have been found at archaeological sites throughout the British Isles. The present quarry was opened in the 1830s producing road setts. The stone was carried by tramway to loading jetties on the shore from where it was taken by ship to Liverpool and other ports. Since the coming of the railway in the 1840s the stone is carried by rail, and is used for rail ballast, road building and the making of concrete. Penmaen-mawr stone has been used in the Mersey Tunnel and the Hamburg by-pass in Germany.

Pen-y-bryn. The tower of this old house is believed to be what's left of the court of Llywelyn Fawr. When bought by the present owners it was used to keep chickens but subsequent research has shown that it dates back to the 13th century. The present building is a Snowdonia cross passage house of about 1553, modernised in 1580 with 'Llywelyn's tower' incorporated into it. Below this house are the remains of an earlier building with three-foot-thick walls, slit windows and a carved mediaeval door and a tunnel, which according to tradition, comes out near the Menai Strait. There are the remains of an Iron Age fort behind the house.

St Bodfan's Church. Named after Bodfan, a son of Helig ap Glanawg of Llys Helig – which is now under the sea, the present church was built in the 1880s, but the original church goes back around a thousand years and was associated with the Welsh princes. There is a circle of yew trees – now listed – in the cemetery which was the site of the old church. The font and the bell – which was installed in 1817 and rung to help people cross the Lafan Sands – is in the present church which closed in 2000. On a wall in the church are plaques to remember families associated with the church, one being the Bond family which had connections with Bond Street in London.

St Bodfan's Church, Abergwyngregyn

St Tegai's Church. It was founded in the late fifth century by Saint Tegai or Saint Cai, the son of Ithel Hael, who came over from Brittany with Saint Cadfan to revive the Christian faith in Wales.

Turnpike. It was erected in around 1825 to serve the Holyhead route built by the Caernarvonshire Turnpike Trust which was founded in 1768. The standard toll was six pence per horse and a carriage with four horses had to pay two shillings. In 1882, local councils took over road maintenance and tolls were abolished.

At one time an old lady looked after this turnpike and one night she heard a knock at the door. She opened it, and to her surprise a bear fell on top of her! The animal's owner helped the old lady to her feet and said that it was a dancing bear and that they were on their way to Cricieth fair. As the bear was too big to go through the small gate that people used, its owner knocked on the door for her to open the large gate. The bear was very tired after walking for miles and was therefore leaning hard on the door – and as the door was opened he fell on top of the old lady!

Ynys Seiriol (Puffin Island). Known in Welsh as Ynys Seiriol, after St Seiriol who established a religious settlement in nearby Penmon in the 6th century. It was later given the name Priestholme by the Vikings. There are the remains of monastic cells hidden by undergrowth on the island. There was once a great colony of puffins here, and at one time they were caught, pickled and sent in barrels to the cities of England where they were considered a delicacy. This and the ever increasing colonies of rats decimated the birds.

Y Wig. At one time it was in the possession of Rhys Fychan, a descendant of Helig ap Glanawg of Llys Helig, who was Richard III's bodyguard. It was with Rhys Fychan that Richard had his last drink of wine. 'Here is to thee Fychan,' he said. 'I will drink to thee, the most faithful Welshman I have ever met in Wales,' and then rushed towards the enemy and was killed. When Henry VIII came to the throne Fychan lost all his lands, including Y Wig. Between Y Wig and the shore is Dalar Hir which was the site of the last battle fought in Gwynedd. Cavalier John Owen of Clenennau was captured by George Twistleton and his Roundheads during the English Civil War. Thirty soldiers were killed in the battle and a 100 prisoners taken.

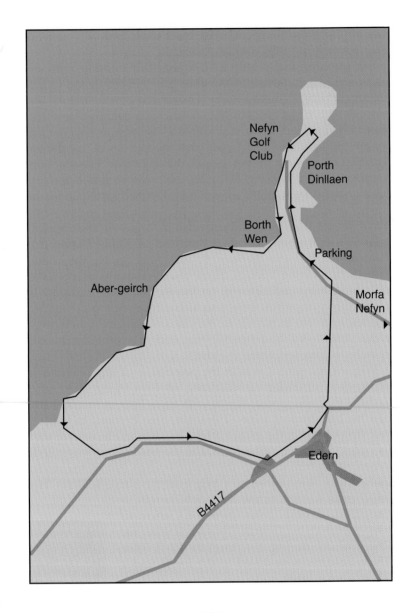

Nefyn Golf Club

Porth Dinllaen

Borth Wen

Parking

Aber-geirch

Morfa Nefyn

Edern

B4417

136

17. Porth Dinllaen

Porth Dinllaen

It was once famous for its shipbuilding. Over 70 ships were built here, with the last, the 149 ton brigantine *Annie Lloyd*, being launched in 1876. It was also a busy port with 7,000 ships calling here in 1804. Coal was one of the main imports, being stored in Warws Dora on the beach. Local produce was exported from here, including pigs and butter. In the mid 1800s, there were plans for Porth dinllaen to be the terminal of the ferry service to Ireland, but the proposal was defeated in parliament by one vote. During the 19th century there was a brickworks here and a landing stage was built on the beach to export the bricks. The Tŷ Coch Inn was, around the 1880s, a naval school kept by a Mrs Jones. The lifeboat station was opened in 1864.

The walk – *from Morfa Nefyn over the headland to Borth Wen and Abergeirch bays and then inland to the village of Edern and back along various paths to Morfa Nefyn.*
5 miles – 3 hours

Park your car in the National Trust car park near the Golf Club in Morfa Nefyn and walk up the hill towards the golf club. Go down the road that runs through the golf course to the shed on the left. There is an unmarked public footpath here across the green to the edge of the cliff – but watch the golf balls! Once you reach the cliff edge, go to your left and follow the path.

At the end of the golf course you will reach a stile near a hut. Go over it and down to **Borth Wen** where a pipe runs to the sea. Cross the footbridge and follow the path up a hill to an old gate. As it won't open, go over it carefully and then bear right keeping to the path that runs above the cliff.

The Nefyn golf course at Porth Dinllaen

Continue towards a kissing gate, and onto **Aber-geirch.** Here there is a signpost. Take the path down to the small bay, over a footbridge and then up the steep steps and continue to another kissing gate. Go through it and continue along the footpath.

Walk down into the bay where there is another signpost, cross the stream, and then up the steep steps to a kissing gate and follow the path above the cliff. Cross another stream to a kissing gate and to a signpost and a gate. Go through the gate and walk inland along the track. If it is wet, you might have to walk on the old bank running alongside it. Continue to a farm gate with a farm on the right. Go through the gate and continue to a road. Turn left and follow the road to the crossroads at Edern near the chapel.

Turn left and walk down towards the pub, over the bridge, up the hill and around the bend where you will see on your left an iron kissing gate. Go through it and up the left hand side of

Tŷ Coch

the field and then down to a gate and kissing gate. Go through the kissing gate, across the track to another kissing gate and up the left hand side of the field to another kissing gate. Continue past the Nefyn Golf Club on your left, down the hill and back to the car park.

If you're feeling thirsty, why not visit the Tŷ Coch Inn on the

Porth Dinllaen life boat station   *Aber-geirch*

beach? Walk out of the car park and turn left and then left again down Lôn Bridin and to the beach. Turn left and walk along the sand towards the houses. A path goes behind the houses which takes you to another beach at Porth Dinllaen where the inn is. You can either return this way, or follow the path behind the inn until you come to a track and then turn left and up the narrow road that crosses the golf course and then downhill to the car park.

OTHER POINTS OF INTEREST

Aber-geirch. From here at one time an undersea telephone cable ran to Ireland. It was about three inches thick, and during the first world war was guarded by soldiers.

Borth Wen was where the *Arjon* from Germany and her crew were all lost in a huge storm in 1863. The villagers, watching the drama unfold from the clifftop, could do nothing to help. The cargo of three ships came ashore here after that storm and the local minister had to warn his flock not to help themselves to the goods.

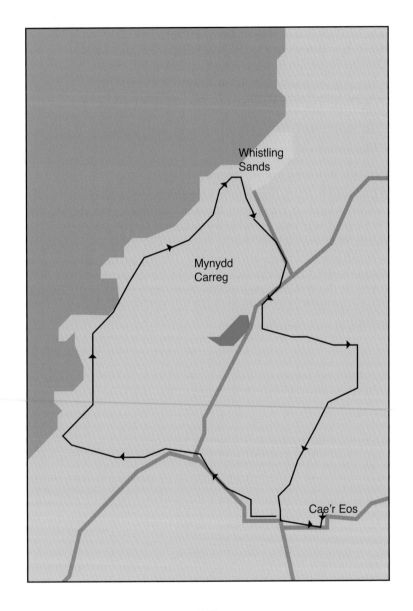

Whistling
Sands

Mynydd
Carreg

Cae'r Eos

18. Porthor

Porthor

It is one of the most popular beaches in Llŷn and gets its English name of 'Whistling Sands' from the grains of sand that rub against each other when pressure is applied such as when someone is walking on them. Many years ago it was used to import coal and lime and to export herring and farm produce. The trade later moved to Porth Ferin where the facilities were better. Two ships were built here during the middle of the 19th century. In 1859, during the great storm that sank the *Royal Charter* off the east coast of Anglesey, nine ships came here to shelter. Two ship were wrecked here in 1879 – the *Sellar* and the *Weaver*. In 1977, the schoolmaster of Aberdaron school was drowned here while trying to rescue one of his pupils, who also drowned.

The walk – *Inland from Porthor and then back to the shore near Porthorion and back to Porthor.*
4 miles – 2 hours

Park your car in the car park at Porthor (there is no bus service here), then walk back up the road and not to the beach. When you reach the junction, turn right and walk along the road until you reach a small forest on your right on the slopes of **Mynydd Carreg.** To the left is a Public Footpath sign, follow it down a narrow track until you come to a 'Private' sign.

There is a kissing gate under an arch to your right. Go through it and across the field to another kissing gate and on to another one and another one until you come to a small wooden bridge and stile. Cross them and up the field and then the field to your right until you come to a gate near caravans.

Go through the gate and past Tŷ Fwg and Ysgubor Fach until you come to a crossroads. You can either turn left and then straight ahead, not following the road to the right, to visit the plaque noting where **Dic Aberdaron** used to live and then return to the crossroads, or turn right and walk along the road until you come to Plasyffordd. Go straight ahead here towards the sea and not right with the road.

You will come to a sharp bend to the left, don't follow it but go through the gate in front of you. Follow the fence on your right until you come to a gate. Go through it and down into a gully near Porthorion, over a small stream and onto a footpath. Follow the path to the right, over another stream, up the path and over a stile. Go straight up until you come to a path that runs alongside a fence and wall.

Follow the path until you come to two kissing gates and a larger gate. Go through the kissing gate nearer the sea and continue until you reach another kissing gate and follow the path back to the car park. Why not rest on Porthor beach? It has lovely sand and a cafe and shop during the summer season.

Porthor

Porthor

OTHER POINTS OF INTEREST

Dic Aberdaron was a noted linguist, speaking, it is said, 13 or 14 languages fluently and with some knowledge of another twenty. They included Latin, Greek, Hebrew, French, Russian, Italian and German – and of course Welsh and English. His father was a carpenter and fisherman and it was assumed that Dic would follow him, but he was more interested in books, and when caught reading would be thrashed by his father. When he was twenty years old, he'd had enough and left home, travelling as far as Liverpool and on a number of occasions as far as London. He would do odd jobs for vicars and men of learning and would receive books as payment. He would walk the

Porthor

country, followed by his numerous cats, in an old army coat with its pockets full of books and on his head either a top hat or a hat made of rabbit fur with its ears sticking up. He also had a French horn which he would blow on entering a town or village. He died in St Asaph, Denbighshire, in 1843 at the age of 63.

Mynydd Carreg. Jasper was once mined here and was exported to be used as building stone, in places such as St James's Palace in London.

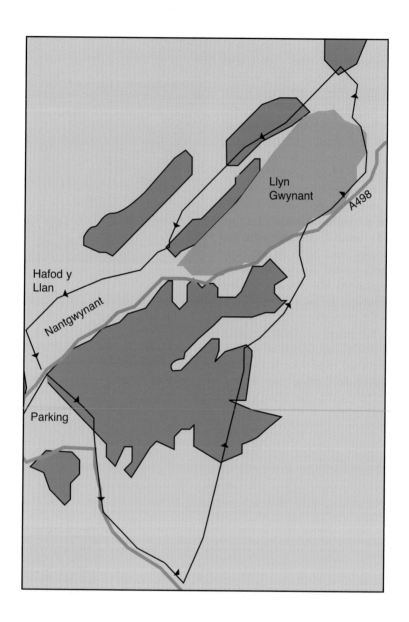

Llyn Gwynant

A498

Hafod y Llan

Nantgwynant

Parking

19. HAFOD Y LLAN

Hafod y Llan farmhouse

The estate includes a third of the summit of Snowdon, twelve tenanted cottages or climbing huts and Y Cnicht. The main farm of the estate, Hafod y Llan, had been the home of the Williams family for fourteen generations. In 1998 Richard Williams decided to sell about four thousand acres (approx 1,600 hectares) of the estate.

The National Trust was successful in a bid to buy the estate in 1998. The Save Snowdon appeal captured the hearts of hundreds of thousands of people worldwide, including the appeal's president, actor Anthony Hopkins, who contributed £1million to help buy Hafod y Llan farm.

The walk – *from Nantgwynant, around Llyn Gwynant and back past Hafod y Llan.*
4.5 miles (km) – 4 hours (if walking around the lake), otherwise 3 miles (km) – 2.6 hours

As there is very little parking space in **Hafod y Llan**, park your car or come off the bus in the Pont Bethania car park near the toilets in **Nantgwynant.** Near the car park and Nantgwynant Lodge is a Public Footpath sign. Go through the gate and up the lane. When you reach a building on your left, the lane forks. Take the left through the trees to a cattle grid.

Don't go over the grid but follow the path with a yellow marker to the right. Go over the bridge and up the path that takes you out of the trees and into a road. Go left and up the hill past a house called Castell on your left. After passing Bryn Bedd on the left, look for 'Public Footpath' signs and a stile, also on the left.

Go over the stile and follow the path running alongside a wall and pine trees to a gate and stile. Go over the stile and follow the path alongside the river to a footbridge. Cross the bridge and follow the path through the rushes, past a white arrow on a large stone and go past a cottage on your right.

Proceed along the path and you will reach another footbridge. Cross the bridge and you will reach a small gate in a wall. Go through it and follow the path alongside the wall. Go through the rhododendron bushes and cross a small stream and on to a stile. Go over the stile and into a pine forest. Cross a small stream and over a stile and follow the path out of the forest. Follow the path straight ahead of you towards a building. You will then see a youth hostel and footpath sign. Go past the building and go straight ahead. You will then see a post in the ground with an arrow pointing left. Disregard it and go straight ahead through the rushes towards a tall tree.

This tree is surrounded by a wall. Go right towards another circular wall with trees within. Go right again and towards a wall that runs down the slope towards Llyn Gwynant. Walk with the wall until you reach a track on your right. Follow the track between two walls, disregarding the lane that goes right.

When the track goes left, go straight ahead with the wall and not along the lane. You will reach the track again but continue to go straight down with the wall until you again come across the track and then follow it down to the road.

Llyn Gwynant

You now have a choice. Either go left and walk back to the car park which is a walk of about half an hour (or catch a bus!) but this won't take you past Hafod y Llan, or go right which will take you around Llyn Gwynant – a walk of about two hours.

If you decide to go around the lake, go right and follow the path which goes alongside the road. When the path ends, look for a stile near the lake. Go over it and follow the path alongside the lake until you come to some trees and a hill. Follow the path up the hill, then down through the trees to a stile. Go over the stile and back to the edge of the lake. Go right rather than along the small beach and follow the track. Then go left into a small car park and camping site. Go right and walk to the far end of the field where there is a bridge.

Cross over the bridge, through a small gate and turn left and follow the path through the rocks to another small gate. Go through it and follow the wall to a stile. Go over the stile and follow the path up through the trees. You will then reach a wooden path. Where the path forks, go right.

You will then reach a large rock – an excellent place to have a picnic – overlooking the lake. Continue along the path until you come to another fork and go up to the right and then down to a gate and stile. Go over the stile and along the flat piece of land following the path, past old copper workings, and to a farm on your left. Continue along the path until you reach a river. Follow the path towards a building on the right and a gate and stile ahead of you. Go over the stile towards a gate and to the left. Go through three more gates, over a bridge and through another three gates near Hafod y Llan farm and then along the lane back to the car park.

OTHER POINTS OF INTEREST

Hafod y Llan. By medieval times this area was parcelled into blocks of land for rough grazing enclosed by crudely built stone walls. By the early 19th century, the upper reaches of land were defined by the *ffridd* walls contouring around the hillside, cutting through the older rough walls and separating the lower and upper reaches of the mountain. These *ffridd* walls suggest enclosures for sheep and cattle. The presence of two field-barns and some dry-stone enclosures are evidence of the harvesting of rough hay on this difficult terrain. Evidence of the self-sufficient farming system of transhumance with the *hafotai* was waning fast by 1800. Better and more substantial farm dwellings were built in the valley by the 18th century to service the whole farm. The older *hafod* or summer dwelling fell into disrepair and the sheep and cattle were increasingly being left to fend for themselves on the hillside as predators disappeared.

The most widespread industrial activity was copper mining from at least the 17th century until the early part of the 20th century. Of the mines on Hafod y Llan, the mine at Cwm Erch is the most important and was surveyed and scheduled by CADW in 1979. Copper mining led to massive and steep inclines, tramways and constructed roads. Ponds were created to serve the mine.

Nantgwynant. The old name for the valley was Nanhwynen or Nan-Hwynan. It used to be more heavily wooded than it is today. The naturalist Edward Lluyd (1660-1709) wrote that "at Nanhwynein trees were so thick that a man on a white horse could not be seen from Llyn Dinas to Pen-y-gwryd, except in two places, and one of these has ever since been called Goleugoed ('lightwood')." At the top of the pass, there remains today a bridge called Pont Goleugod.

Nantgwynant is about seven miles long, with Llyn Gwynant about one and a half miles, and up to 50 feet deep. A flat expanse of meadow stretching above the lake suggests it was much longer at one time.

Y Gŵr Blew (the hairy man). Wales has its own yeti or bigfoot and it lives in Nantgwynant! Some say that he was the son of a prince which had come to attack the people of Nantgwynant and that he had been left behind. As he was living wild, a thick covering of hair grew all over his body. He lived by stealing from houses during the night. Everyone knew that it was y *Gŵr Blew* that stole their property but they had no idea where he lived. One night, a young wife had been left alone in her house called Ty'n-'rowallt as her husband had gone away to buy a cow. Suddenly, she heard glass breaking and she rushed towards the window with her husband's sword. She saw a large, hairy hand coming through the window – y *Gŵr Blew.* She raised the sword above her head and brought it smashing down on the hand. The creature let out a loud scream which was heard all over the valley.

The husband had heard the scream and he rushed home but by then his neighbours had arrived and they all decided to go and look for y *Gŵr Blew.* Outside the house, in the snow, was a large, hairy hand, covered in blood, and there was a trail of blood running from the house. They followed the trail up the slope of Snowdon until they came to a waterfall. There they saw a cave with the trail of blood leading into it. Nobody wanted to enter the cave so they dammed the stream and water started to flow into the cave. Suddenly, y *Gŵr Blew* jumped out and ran up the slope over Y Lliwedd. Everyone fired their arrows at him but he escaped. A few days later, someone saw him hiding in a large crack in a rock near Maen Du'r Arddu. They went up there, but he had seen them coming and had run away, over Snowdon, down Cwm Llan and over Y Cnicht. Some say that he still lives in a cave somewhere in the area.

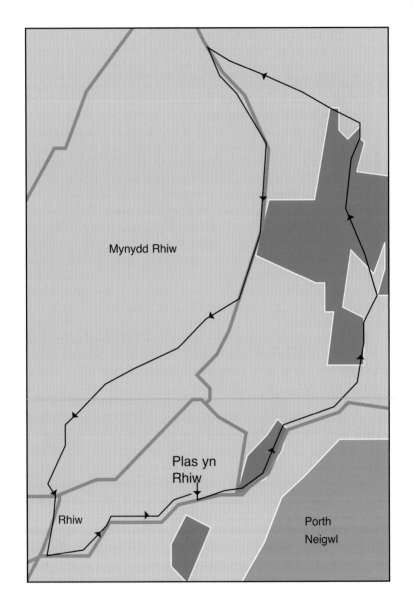

20. Plas yn Rhiw

Tel. 01758 780219

Plas yn Rhiw

Plas yn Rhiw is a small 16th century manor house with Georgian additions which was rescued and restored by the three Keating sisters who bought it in 1938. It has ornamental gardens with many interesting flowering trees and shrubs. Carpets of snowdrops and bluebells can be seen in the wood above the house in spring. The poet R. S. Thomas lived in Sarn Plas on the estate for a few years after he retired from being rector of Aberdaron.

The walk – *from Plas yn Rhiw to Porth Neigwl and then along footpaths and narrow lanes reaching the road that takes you to Rhiw and then back downhill to Plas yn Rhiw.*
7.5 miles – 2.5 hours

Plas yn Rhiw

Park your car in Plas yn Rhiw. (There is a bus service to Rhiw, and you can start the walk from there.) After visiting the house, walk out of the grounds and go down the hill until you reach the bottom with a caravan park on your right and a farm on your left.

You will then come to a Public Footpath sign on your right which leads you over a stile to **Porth Neigwl.** It will take you about ten minutes to go to the beach from here – well worth a visit.

Otherwise, carry on along the road until you come to another Public Footpath sign and the sign to Ty'n Parc. Follow this path or track, past Ty'n Parc and into a pine forest. Carry on past some sheds on your right until you come to a clear patch in the forest and a track running into it from the left. Go straight ahead along a narrow path towards a white house until you come to a gate.

Go through the gate and up the path through the brambles behind a house called Tyddyn Corn until you come to another gate. Go through it and up the track, then left through the trees. Go out of the trees and near a gate take the track to its left (i.e. the one in the middle). Past the white house on the left and go up the path to the right to a gate and a broken stile. Go through the gate and walk alongside the wall until you come to two houses on your left.

Turn left past the nearest house until you come to a track and follow it to the right until you come to a cattle grid and a tarmaced road. Go past two houses on your left until you come to a junction and a telephone kiosk. Turn left and up the hill past a stile on your left to the top of the hill where there is a magnificent view to your left of Porth Neigwl and the southern

Llŷn coast. To your right is **Mynydd Rhiw.**

Carry on until you come to, on your right, a gate, a corrugated iron shed and a stone stile. Go over the stile and follow the track to the left until you come to two gates and a stile to their right. Go over the

Bwlch

stile and follow the path that eventually turns into a track and then joins another track and forward towards some houses. Walk towards the gate, go through it and near a house called Hirael you will reach a crossroads. Turn left and then right at the next crossroads and into Rhiw.

Walk past the village hall on your right and to the crossroads. Turn left and go down the hill towards Porth Neigwl. After walking a few minutes you will see **Bwlch** cottage on your left. Carry on down the hill and near the bottom, on your left, you will see the sign to Plas yn Rhiw and return to your car

OTHER POINTS OF INTEREST

Bwlch, formerly known as Bwlch y Rhiw – was the home of Morgan Griffith or Morgan y Gogrwr (the sieve maker) who was an 18th century nonconformist preacher. At that time every preacher had to be licensed by the church – and Griffith was not. He was twice caught preaching in the fields and the second time was taken to court in Pwllheli. To try and get him a lighter sentence, his brother in law brought his two children – in baskets on a mule – to the courthouse but to no avail. Because his children could read, it was assumed that he was teaching them 'bad things'. Griffith was found guilty and sent to the navy. Sometime in the early 1740s he was put on the *Colchester* which was anchored in the Thames. Britain was at war with France at the time and the *Colchester* went up to Scotland to patrol the waters there. Conditions were very bad on the ship and eventually Griffith, like many others, died and was buried at sea.

Mynydd Rhiw. There are the remains of a Neolithic stone axe factory on its northern slope, a burial chamber on its eastern side and the remains of an old homestead on the southern side. There are old manganese mines at the foot of the mountain, where over 60,000 tons of ore were mined during the second world war. It was taken by an aerial ropeway to a pier on the shore. During the beginning of the 20th century (especially in 1912, during the Russian/Japanese war), this area produced 90% of Britain's manganese, employing 200 men. It was used to harden steel in Brymbo, north-eastern Wales, and was used in the production of armaments. At the end if the 19th century, the ore would be carried in small trucks to a stream where it would be washed by women and then transported on sledges to Porth Neigwl to be loaded onto ships. On the top of the hill is a radio station tracking missiles which are fired from Aberporth on the Ceredigion coast.

Porth Neigwl (or Hell's Mouth) – has seen numerous shipwrecks over the centuries. In 1629 a French ship carrying members of the aristocracy, lured by lights carried by wreckers on the shore, hit the rocks. It is said that the locals attacked the survivors, killing them and cutting their fingers and ears off to get at the jewellery. Two local men were hanged for this foul deed. In 1865, an Austrian ship carrying corn went on the rocks and its cargo was spread over the area. It is said that local farms gathered it all up and fed it to their pigs. In 1898, a ship called *The Twelve Apostles*, which had been built at Pwllheli in 1858, was blown ashore and the captain's message to Lloyds of London read 'Twelve Apostles taking water in Hell's Mouth'.

Porth Neigwl

The crew managed to get into a small boat but got into difficulties. The maid of nearby Trefollwyn saw them and waded into the stormy water to help bring the boat ashore. Such is the ferocity of the weather at Porth Neigwl that during the last century a paint manufacturer put up painted frames on the eastern end of the bay to test the durability of the paint. These frames have now either corroded or fallen into the sea.

TO BE PUBLISHED IN 2007

National Trust Walks

2. Central and Southern Wales

DOROTHY HAMILTON

Llygad Gwalch